C0-DAL-076

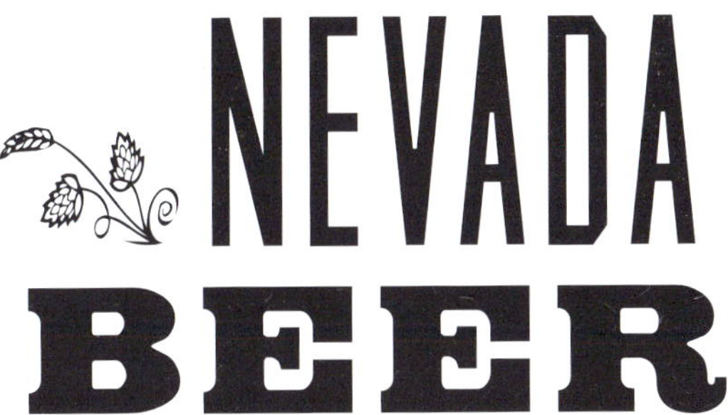
NEVADA
BEER

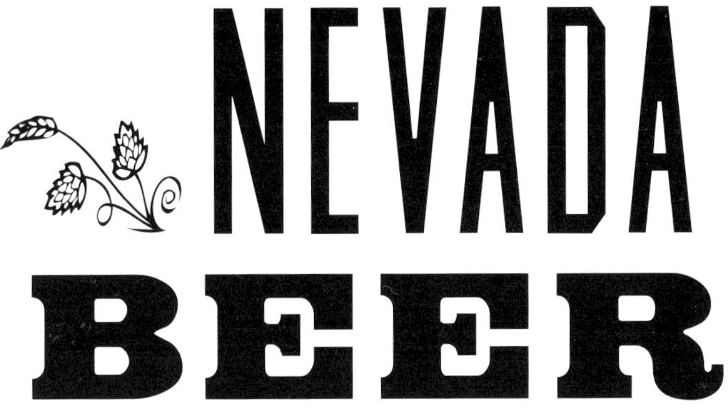

An Intoxicating History

PAT EVANS

Foreword by Great Basin Brewing founder Tom Young

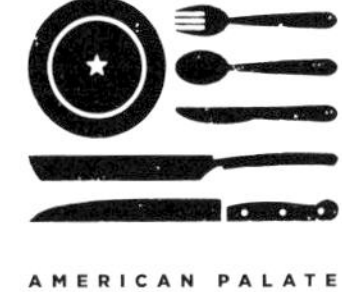

AMERICAN PALATE

Published by American Palate
A Division of The History Press
Charleston, SC
www.historypress.com

Front cover: Red Rock Canyon, Nevada. *The Carol M. Highsmith Archive, Library of Congress, Prints and Photographs Division.*

First published 2018

Manufactured in the United States

ISBN 9781467140447

Library of Congress Control Number: 2018952984

Notice: The information in this book is true and complete to the best of our knowledge. It is offered without guarantee on the part of the author or The History Press. The author and The History Press disclaim all liability in connection with the use of this book.

CONTENTS

FOREWORD

Nevada was settled by innovators. The first were the brave Native Americans whose tenacity, tools and traditions of civilization enabled them to thrive in a seemingly harsh and dry environment. The second wave of newcomers, fueled by news of discoveries of gold and silver, came searching for a fortuitous new start in life. These trailblazers were driven by a variety of passions, yet all were impelled by an independent spirit, a bold, burning desire and want or need to seek new ground and the creative pursuit of celebrating life through independence. The region has steadfastly been recognized for its enormous beauty—sweeping valleys and towering mountains separated by expanses of rugged terrain. The Basin and Range landscape was, and continues to be, molded from shifting continental plates that pushed and pulled the land and now stretch the region from the majestic Sierra Nevada range on the west to the Wasatch Front beyond Salt Lake City to the east. The vast Great Basin is a land where all rivers flow in but none flow out, terminating before reaching an ocean. It is dry land but bears comforting lakes within the high desert terrain in the north and colorful warmer desert in the south. The raw splendor offers solitude to the adventurers who choose to bask in its chiseled splendor.

I began my adult working career as an exploration and mining geologist. When I was having difficulty in deciding on a college major, a fellow student told me that geologists got paid to hike, solve exciting problems and travel to exotic places. Being especially adventuresome, I dove in and was intrigued to learn about earth processes and how small of a speck in time we humans have occupied in this voyage we call life. Working as a geologist is highly relevant to starting and running a brewery. When searching for gold—more often than not—one is most often unsuccessful. The result—discovering where gold isn't instead of discovering where it is. Resilience is essential when navigating the road to accomplishment. The ability to get back up time and time again after being knocked down gives folks loads more chances to succeed. Tenacity, I believe, is perhaps a most valuable trait when starting an endeavor or business, especially when there were few standards to mimic. Moreover, geologists traditionally drink lots of beer—kind of a job requisite. I was an avid homebrewer for many years, winning many accolades at local and national competitions. This boosted my brewing knowledge and fortified my confidence.

In the late 1980s, I was the on-site manager of a soon-to-be-opened California gold mine. Although we had just finished the onerous permitting process, just before we broke ground, my employer abruptly decided to sell all its mines to generate cash to bail out one of the failing companies it controlled. I was downsized against my will. This builds character, as the door hits you on the ass as you lock it for the last time. On the heels of this perceived setback, I resolved that beer would carry me on to the next expedition.

The task of opening a brewery was more monumental than I had imagined. Entrepreneurs are optimists. It's in our DNA. We often ask, "How are we going to do this?" before we asked the more pertinent questions: "Why are we doing this?" and "Can this be done?" Nevada had and still has some of the toughest laws restricting what a want-to-be brewer can do. Dick Murray, a guy who didn't drink but wanted to start a brewery, was actively seeking to change Nevada laws. Along with Murray, a group, including me, offered assistance, somewhat out of curiosity, but all with an inkling that we might want to start a brewery. Murray never did attempt to start a brewery. My initial plan was to open a small production brewery, but the new Nevada law, when it was finally enacted, contained numerous restrictions, including production limits. These made it more advantageous to operate a brewpub than a production brewery that, if successful, would be forced to cease production when the arbitrary limit was reached (then, five thousand barrels in Washoe County; one barrel = thirty-one gallons). We brewers have made some progress over the years through gallant efforts, but it has been painfully slow and costly. Much more needs to be done on the legislative front. Brewers in other states and other nations where there are no production limits and with more favorable distribution options have clear advantages over Nevada brewers.

In addition to changing state laws, local city and county ordinances needed to be changed. These were easier to obtain than state allowances, as the local elected officials were very excited to bring brewing back to Nevada. Additionally, regulators from many agencies needed to be educated about the operation of a brewery, an endeavor that ultimately consumed a great deal of time and took serious and nearly fatal cuts out of our dwindling cash reserves.

When deciding to move forward with our brewing dreams, I have to offer gratitude for the trust my wife, Bonda, offered. We had two young daughters in grade school, and she was understandably reluctant to dedicate all of our life's savings that we had both worked very hard for to a beer dream. Breweries are capital-intensive. We pledged every spare dime to the project, but that wasn't enough. We convinced some thirsty investors to contribute and applied for a loan at every bank in Nevada. Each one turned us down, probably wisely, due to the lack of comparable businesses in the state and our inexperience. We finally managed to secure about a quarter of the funds from a California bank that specialized in risky loans to entrepreneurs backed by U.S. government funds. This did require lots and lots of collateral, including pledging our personal residence. We formed a team that ultimately carved our road, including business partner Camille Prenn, who was also in the mining business, and my longtime friend and fellow home-brewer Eric McClary. Eric and I made a good team. With my master's degree in engineering and discipline of calculating everything to the umpteenth decimal point, Eric's degree in film lent great artistic talent. Eric succumbed to Parkinson's disease far too early in his life, though his legacy lives on in our tradition of fine handcrafted beers.

We opened the doors, not because we were ready to, but because we were totally broke, mostly because of misdirection caused by our own inexperience and delays imposed by suspicious regulators. Thanks to thirsty and trusting Nevadans, we've been crowded since day one. We certainly needed the money that these curious Nevadans brought, but more importantly, we needed a base of enthusiastic imbibers to enjoy our brewing efforts; they have now become friends.

In the early '90s, Nevadans were starved for quality beer. The large national brewers found it most profitable and efficient to brew beers that went far out of their way not to offend anyone and were of low enough alcohol content to ensure increased and higher consumption. They spent far more on the advertising budget than they did to brew beer. The problem was that while their beer offered little to offend anyone, there was nothing in the beer to please anyone. The quest for taste opened the door for eager craft brewers to fill the flavor void. Today, I saw a billboard boasting, "A majority of drinkers agree that Miller Lite has more taste than Bud Light." Really? 100 percent of drinkers would agree that craft beer has more taste than any "Lite" beer. Game over—craft beer wins again.

Nevadans continue to be opinionated, discerning and demanding. In response, Nevada brewers continue to produce world-class beers and innovations that stretch brewing boundaries. At Great Basin, we were always brewers first, driven by a fanatical passion to brew the best beers known on this planet, keeping the virtues of integrity and a keen pioneering spirit alive. We are grateful to have gained the trust of the patrons who have enjoyed our beers with us for the past twenty-five years. We will continue to work hard to hold on to it. Setting high standards builds confidence in our patrons. Heartfelt community service is an integral part of our commitment. At Great Basin, we truly believe that it is our duty as brewers to try to "make this world a better place, one pint at a time."

Beer unites! The world turns on a smoother path with beer, for a long time an elixir for conversations. Beer transcends gender, ethnicity, most religious beliefs, political persuasion, mood and age group. I truly believe that as we navigate within our own private worlds, beer, when consumed in moderation, paves the road for the sharing of ideas and thoughts to bring consensus in an all too frequently turbulent society. If each of us would spend just a few more minutes a day expressing our thoughts, ideas, dreams and desires to loved ones, friends and family, harmony would become more achievable. Romance has been won and lost, family traditions have been established, friendships have been formed, careers have found direction, difficult decisions have been made, and all the while, the spirit of friendship and community has been reinforced. At Great Basin's restaurants/taproom and at other Nevada breweries, we see this happen every day.

Perhaps the most satisfying reward of my years at Great Basin Brewing Company has been the absolute joy we have been awarded by being a small part of the lives of our staff members, our loyal but picky and discerning enthusiasts and the community that has supported us as we have supported them. Nevada's craft beer industry follows many other pioneers, started by the wise men and women who brewed beers before us, be it for necessary sustenance or for the celebration of achievement and of life. Pioneers brewed beer in boom and bust Nevada mining towns where gold and silver were the foundation but beer was essential. Today's pioneers brew beer to fill an essential void, and we are proud to do our part.

Nevada Beer will not only chronicle Nevada's brewing history but will take its rightful place in the Silver State's history as well. Like the origins of our fine state's craft beer industry itself, Pat Evans recognized that this story would fill missing chapters of Nevada's history in a place so rugged and magnificent that the glass will forever be half full.

Today, we celebrate innovation and exploration—the forces that move us forward. We raise our glass to those who have blazed the beer trails for us and trust that those who follow us will respect our contribution to the craft. We will always brew from the heart to offer excitement and promise. French author André Gide ounce wrote, "Follow those who seek the truth, but run like hell from those who claim to have found the truth." As we trek through this journey called life, we must always walk with an open mind. Let's observe and celebrate the wonders, both big and small, that we meet on our journeys.

—Tom Young
Founder of Great Basin Brewing Company

PREFACE

As I was preparing to move out to Las Vegas from Grand Rapids, Michigan, an often-lauded beer city, I heard it time and time again: "What are you going to do? The beer sucks out there."

I wrote the book on Grand Rapids beer and still maintain a column in *Grand Rapids Magazine*, as I head back regularly for writing work. The city and Michigan as a whole have a renowned beer scene. It had me a tad worried. I'd only been to Nevada twice before, once a few weeks prior, and hadn't found much in the means of local beer.

I told my publishing editor I was moving, and he put me in touch with the Nevada editor, who said they were looking for someone to write a history of Nevada beer. I didn't know anything about the state's beer scene, so why not? It would be a great way to dive right in, get to know the community and learn about the history of Nevada—which was, and still is, fascinating to me.

I saw a count of fewer than forty breweries in the state and a relatively short time in statehood. Well, this shouldn't take long. I committed to a quick turnaround. While I accomplished the task, it was silly of me to think it would be easy.

First, while the history of Nevada is surprisingly well documented for having so many ghost towns and being part of the Wild West, those ghost towns all had breweries, and most were not at all well documented. It did teach me all sorts of awesome facts about the Wild West that didn't fit the book though! It wasn't all that wild and in some respects was decidedly cosmopolitan.

Second, the breweries that do call Nevada home are amazing and have quite the backstories, enough so that the extent of them all don't fit in one book. Many have been short-changed. Almost every one of these breweries in this state brews at least one great beer, if not multiple. The chances of walking into one of Nevada's breweries and having an undrinkable or bad beer are so much smaller than those states with hundreds of breweries—a statement I truly didn't think I'd be able to make when I started this project.

Third, it was also foolish of me to believe all the brewers would welcome me with open arms and spill their life stories to me. Many did, some of whom certainly could be more standoffish than they are, such as Tom Young at Reno's Great Basin and Dave Pascual at Las Vegas's Big Dog's. I challenge anyone to find two nicer humans than those two.

More than anything though, I've discovered awesome side stories that have necessitated an auxiliary website, NevadaBrews.com.

Six months is how quickly I pulled this book together, and I'm proud of it. However, there are so many people, places and breweries I can dive into much more deeply, not to mention issues, like the pay-to-play issue, which I'm not entirely sure anyone in Nevada is fully clear on.

As this is published, I'm just a year into my life in Nevada, and there's still so much to learn, beer and otherwise. I'm hoping those who read this—and more—will join me on that site.

ACKNOWLEDGEMENTS

Writing a book is never easy, but without these people, this book wouldn't have been possible:

Mom and Dad back in Grand Rapids, because, well, I wouldn't be here otherwise.

My brother Tory for making sense of time commitments.

The beautiful, talented and supportive Alyssa, because without her and the Vegas Golden Knights, I wouldn't be in Nevada.

Laurie Krill at The History Press for suggesting the idea of writing this book before I had even moved to Nevada.

Michael Borer, the UNLV professor who opened his arms to me as soon as I got to Las Vegas and helped introduce me to the beer scene and became a great friend.

Likewise, Bob Barnes, who's given me a place to write in Las Vegas, filled me in on the local scene upon arrival and is a true steward of Nevada beer.

Tom Young at Great Basin for showing nothing short of the greatest hospitality when I visited Reno and, of course, writing my foreword.

And the rest of the brewers of Nevada who were welcoming to the idea of an outsider coming into the scene to help promote it and tell its story.

PART I

EARLY NEVADA

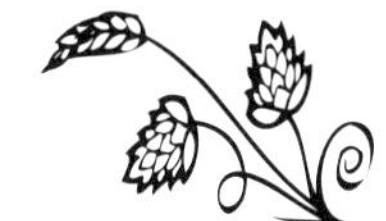

CHAPTER 1

GHOST BREWERIES

Mining was hard work, certainly guaranteed to make the workers thirsty after a hard day of labor. Early Nevada was full of beer. As the population of Nevada swelled with increasing discoveries of gold and silver, so, too, did the need for beer and other indulgences. Towns popped up and disappeared just as quickly. As did breweries, which helps make the history of Nevada beer particularly fascinating. The state's mining boom height in the late nineteenth century was also its pre-Prohibition beer height. In 1880, there were more than thirty-five breweries in the state making more than 13,900 barrels of beer. (In 2015, Nevada's thirty-four breweries brewed 64,901 barrels.) Many of those breweries are in cities that no longer exist, places lost to history with little more than remnants of building foundations. Long gone as well are many of the histories of those beer makers, with all that remains from some being names and records of how much was made.

As was the truth in much of the rest of America, Germans constituted a significant number of immigrants coming to find a new life in Nevada in the 1800s. And just as with the rest of the nation, many of those Germans found a need for one of their classic industries: brewing. If hard physical labor in a mine wasn't up their alley, maybe hard physical labor in a brewhouse was.

In the modern ideals of brewing, the first brewery in Nevada was started before the area was even a territory. A major rush occurred in 1859 to Washoe, which brought with it a boon in breweries.

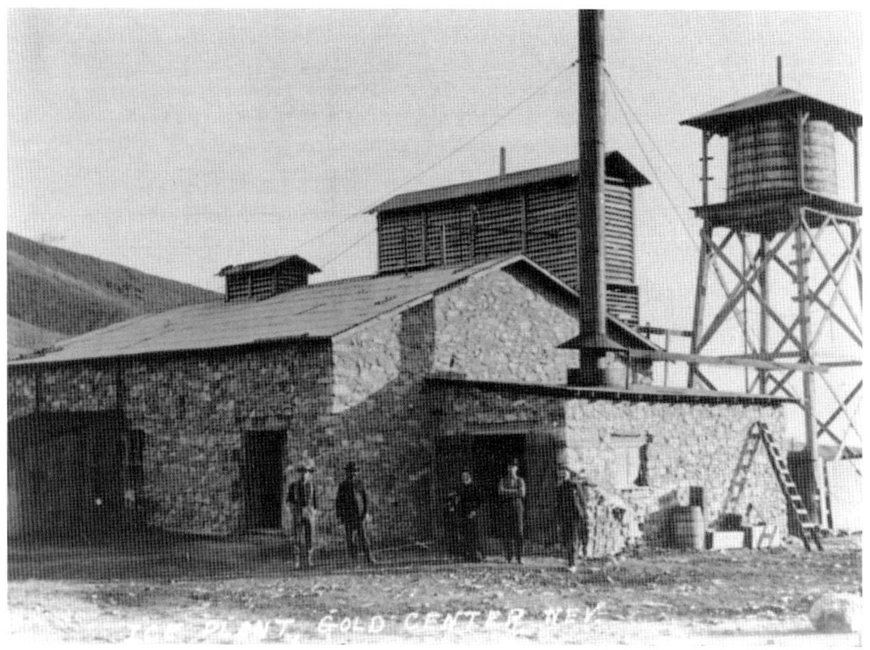

Many of Nevada's early breweries didn't leave much by way of records or building remains. This is Gold Center Ice and Brewing Company; all that remains is the foundation in the ghost town of Gold Center, near Beatty. *Courtesy UNLV Libraries Special Collections.*

The 1860 census of Nevada listed three German brewers in the Comstock area. Union Brewery, Nevada Brewery, St. Louis Brewery, Washoe Brewery and Philadelphia Brewery all generally showed up as the most popular throughout the years.

The Nevada Brewery was in a two-story building in Virginia City and, according to an article in a 1972 *Reno Gazette-Journal*, stayed open until 1913. The Nevada Brewery seems to have been a waypoint of sorts, often offering a sense of location in many newspaper reports. Still, it made the news occasionally, like this 1875 report in the *Pioche Record*, reciting the seemingly stereotyping *Gold Hill News*:

> *While the driver of the Nevada Brewery wagon was moving a keg of beer in front of Piper's saloon, Virginia, on Saturday, the bung got loose and the beer flew around in all directions, to the great amusement of the spectators and the disgust of the driver. When asked how the accident happened, he replied: "Vell, I don't vas know exactly how dam tings vas happens. I shust vas roll dem parrels arount aboud a leedle, ven I dinks I makes dem*

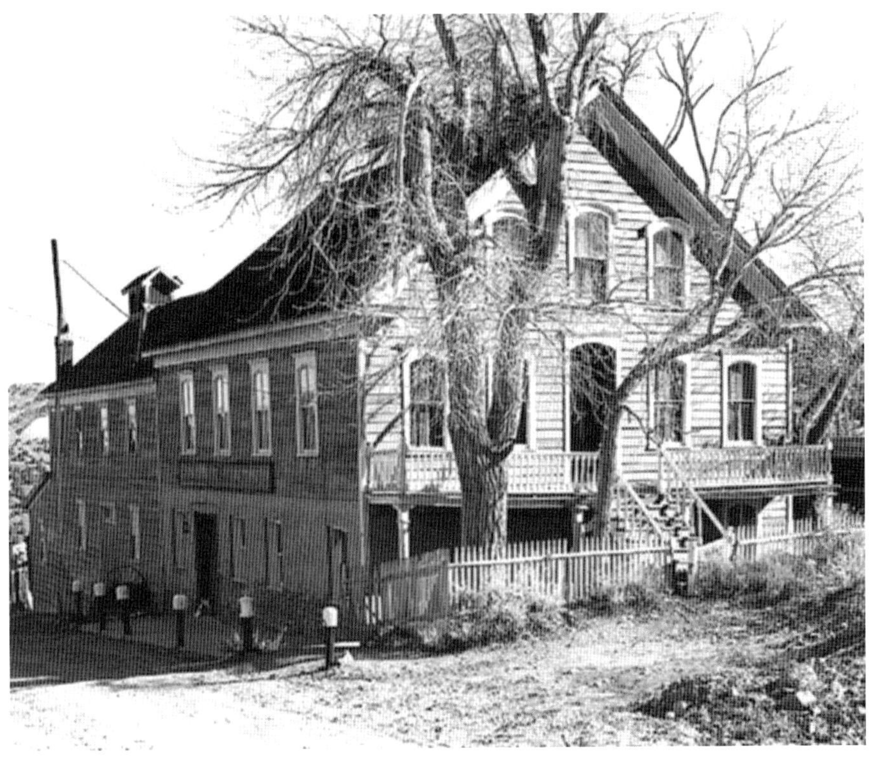

Nevada Brewery was one of the first recorded brewing operations in Nevada. Nevada Brewery stayed open from 1860 to 1913 and was often a point of reference in newspaper articles. *Courtesy Nevada Historical Society.*

> *pungholes loose from dem plugs, unt der peer makes dem ous, unt spurt all rount. Gott fur tam der heissen wetter."*

Most breweries in Nevada's history have been small operations, leaving very little behind besides a few newspaper mentions here and there. While plenty opened up, few lasted more than a year or two, although California Brewery in Virginia City lasted more than twenty years. In true Wild West fashion, intoxicated miner Tony King stabbed California Brewery co-owner Joe Black because he refused to sell beer to the drunkard.

Then there are the two dominant pre-Prohibition breweries, Carson Brewing and Reno Brewing, both of which left a wealth of information.

CHAPTER 2

A GLIMPSE AT EARLY NEVADA

The Comstock Lode, which spurred the 1859 rush, was a massive cache of silver ore that created the most palpable excitement of the West since the California gold rush ten years earlier and helped separate most of the area now making up the state of Nevada, which previously was part of the Utah Territory. This led to statehood in 1864. The long-lasting lode led to mining camps developing into the thriving urban centers of Virginia City and Gold Hill.

With those urban centers came very cosmopolitan cities, according to Ronald James, who spent more than three decades as the Nevada state historic preservation officer and is author of more than a dozen books, many on the history of the state. "The intermountain West tended to create island settlements in vast open landscapes, but those settlements were instant cities," James said. "There's a whole lot of places where people don't live; you can't really have rural in Nevada."

At its peak in the 1870s, Virginia City had an estimated population of 25,000 residents, a number that dropped to 500 in the middle of the twentieth century and rose again to 855 in 2010. Its population led Nevada to statehood in 1864, the thirty-sixth state admitted to the Union. Once called the richest city in America, Virginia City included complex gas and sewer lines, brick homes, theaters, an opera house and three daily newspapers, according to the *History of the Comstock Lode*, a 1943 book by Grant Smith.

The wealth that the silver and gold strike created in Comstock led to Virginia City becoming a sister city of sorts to San Francisco, an international hub already at the time, and allowed Virginia City to import the best of the

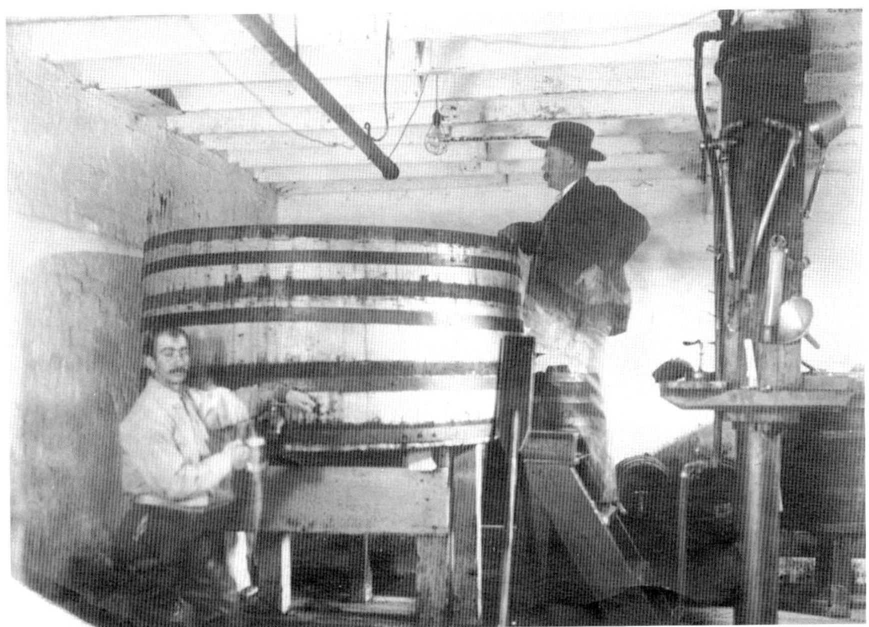

Albert Schnitzer oversees a batch of beer in the brewing process at Virginia City Brewery. *Courtesy Nevada Historical Society.*

best, James said. Connections made in the city allowed for Parisian fashion, Chesapeake Bay oysters and European beers.

Miners in Virginia City worked hard but were handsomely rewarded. Working eight-hour shifts, the highest-paid miners saw $4.00 per day, James said. A contemporary worker at the Colt Armory factory in Connecticut would make $1.25 for a ten- to twelve-hour day.

"It is fair to say that Comstock miners, some of the best paid in the industrial world, would have demanded the best," James said. "The Comstock had it all."

James noted an establishment in the early West might have had "brewery" in the name but would not actually produce any beer. Instead, a business such as Hibernia Brewery and Saloon had the word "brewery" as an indicator that it served fresh beer on tap rather than bottles. Most of the breweries, if not all, at the time also lacked taprooms, so those particular brewery saloon establishments were the sole places to taste a fresh draught beer, served on contract with the real breweries producing the beer.

Virginia City residents boasted more than one hundred saloons at its height, many of which were family-friendly and the antithesis of the dramatized Wild West saloon.

James was part of a team that excavated four saloon sites in Virginia City, all of which operated between 1862 and 1885 and give perhaps the best glimpse into saloon life in early Nevada. The teams in Virginia City were looking for saloons, but the four excavated saloon sites cannot be compared to any other community because there aren't any other sites so well documented.

James wrote in his book *The Roar and the Silence: A History of Virginia City and the Comstock Lode* that Virginia City and Gold Hill residents consumed 75,000 gallons of liquor and 225,000 gallons of beer in 1880. Among the most prominent bottles at all the establishments were Glasgow ale bottles from Scotland, proving these weren't backwater camps but true international cosmopolitan cities. Along with beer, wine, port and champagne were common. For the hard stuff, gin and whiskey seemed to reign supreme, while ginger beer and soda water bottles also were common, likely meant for mixing.

In the excavations, James said there was a noticeable tendency for the Irish saloon to have more whiskey bottles. The whiskies were not moonshine, and while he has no authority on the absolute quality, James said the bottles were well crafted and embossed, suggesting whiskey of quality and unlikely to be "rot-gut spirits." "I would expect that sort of poor whiskey in some western backwater, but the Comstock represented wealth," James said.

The excavations also uncovered imported mineral water from Germany at a German saloon and a carbon water filter from London, James said.

Virginia City was far from the only mining boomtown, but it is perhaps the best documented, largely because it still exists as a city, albeit at a stature much smaller than it once was. Mark Twain wrote a book, *Roughing It*, in part about his time in Virginia City, and James said, "No tour of the world or continent was complete without a visit to Virginia City." President Ulysses S. Grant and his family made a stop in Virginia City as part of his post-presidency world tour, as did many international travelers.

While Virginia City was the early driver, a little to the north, Reno developed into the metropolitan center of upper Nevada—along with the state capital of Carson City—while other cities failed to grow to significant size in the harsh climate of the state. Nevada, it should be noted, is the thirty-fifth most populated state and ninth least densely populated while being the second most urbanized, behind New Jersey. Most of Nevada's population lives in Reno and Las Vegas, while the rest of the state is largely empty land.

Booze was prominent in Nevada, but an aside in several documents was the arrival of the Chinese immigrants in Nevada, noting the arrival brought with it the spread of opium to the general population.

The largest brewery at the time was Jacob Klein's Carson City Brewery, which brewed more than 2,071 barrels in 1880. A Virginia City operation led by Franklin & Schroeder brewed more than 1,500 barrels of beer, while Rapp & Langan brewed nearly 1,000 barrels following a year in which the company brewed 1,179.

As the Comstock Lode was depleted, Nevada's population began to wane. Luckily, another large strike was hit in the first few years of the twentieth century in Tonopah and Goldfield, propping up the state. A few of the mining cities survived solely by becoming county seats, like Austin and Eureka. Virginia City, meanwhile, boomed and then nearly disappeared before reinventing itself as a "bohemian and artistic enclave" and a tourist destination, in part thanks to the mid-twentieth-century television show *Bonanza*.

Some sources said the life expectancy of a mining town was less than three years. "That's a byproduct of mining; unlike agriculture, it's nonrenewable, and there's no reason for people to stay once they're gone," James said. "The economic engine of a lot of the West was mining, and take mining out of it, as happened, and the doldrums of the industry and the state almost disappeared as the population had dropped so dramatically."

James said Nevada was the only state to see national voices suggest changing it back to a territory, in the 1920s, but it was quickly sustained by the construction of the Hoover Dam and legalization of gambling and short-term divorces.

CHAPTER 3

EARLY BREWERIES

While the early days of Nevada were littered with breweries, the state's beer industry was captured by two main breweries as it matured: Carson Brewing and Reno Brewing Company, both of which were able to grow to a significant size and survive past Prohibition.

Two Nevada historians embraced the state's early beer history in the 1980s, well before the beer boom of the late 1990s and early twenty-first century. Eric Moody and Robert Nylen documented the early Nevada beer industry in *Brewed in Nevada* and articles and exhibitions through the Nevada State Museum.

As with most industries, beer was local in the nineteenth and early twentieth centuries, as noted by the many brand names, such as Tahoe, Mount Rose and Sierra beers produced by early breweries. In 1863, men by the name of Ploshke and Betz opened the Pioneer in Austin, Nevada, making Pioneer Beer.

By 1880, there were breweries spread across the state. Most were small, but some were large enough that they would be of significant size in the modern beer industry. Breweries were located in Aurora, Austin, Battle Mountain, Belleville, Carson City, Elko, Esmerelda, Eureka, Gold Hill, Grantsville, Halleck, Hamilton, Paradise Valley, Pioche, Reno, Silver City, Tuscarora, Tybo, Virginia City, White Pine and Winnemucca. Carson City, Elko, Pioche, Tuscarora and Winnemucca each necessitated two breweries; Virginia City had four (Nevada, Virginia, Union and California); and Eureka

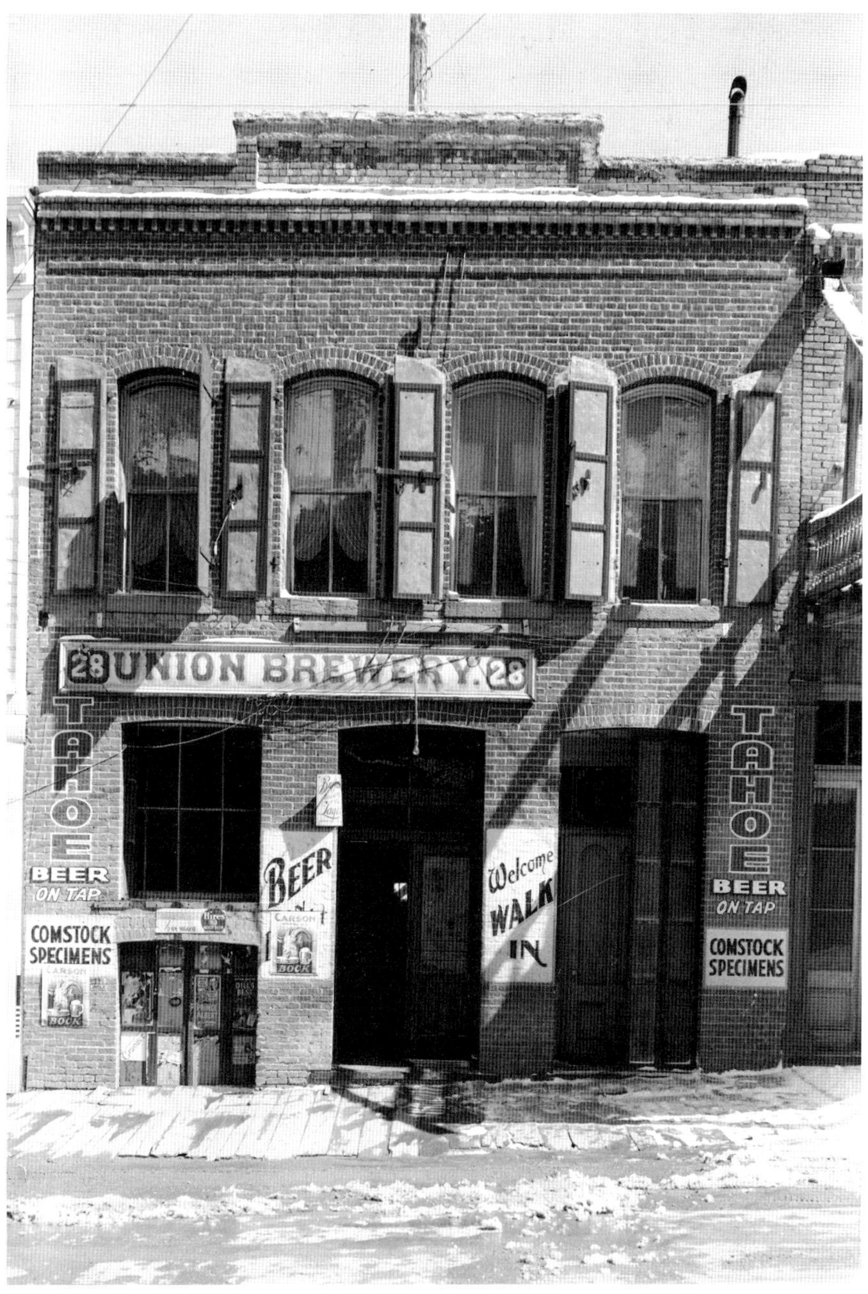

Union Brewery in Virginia City. Note the advertisement for Tahoe Beer. Often, "breweries" were taprooms with contracts to serve a brewery's beer. *Courtesy Library of Congress.*

had five, including the Lautenschlager operation, which brewed more than 1,200 barrels of beer in 1880.

It should be noted that in 1880, Great Britain had 26,114 breweries, Germany had 23,940 and the United States had 3,293, just a tad more than France's 3,100.

The same "article" that stated these facts included this line, referring to George Becker's Pacific beer: "The best one in the whole lot is in Reno, and Geo. Becker is the proprietor. No beer in the world can come up to that made by Becker."

One of the breweries in Tuscarora was underground, along a path miners would take to get home. They would stop and fill buckets full of the beer before continuing their journey.

Winnemucca provided a particularly fierce rivalry between two breweries on the same street, Bridge Street, as Winnemucca City Brewery and Empire Brewery both sought customers in the city boosted as a stop on the Central Pacific Railroad.

One of the Winnemucca beer entrepreneurs, Charles Kesler, is reported as saying, "This young state is the thirstiest in the union!" Kesler ran the Empire Brewery, an establishment that brewed with great velocity its first several years in business, even with Winnemucca City Brewery nearby.

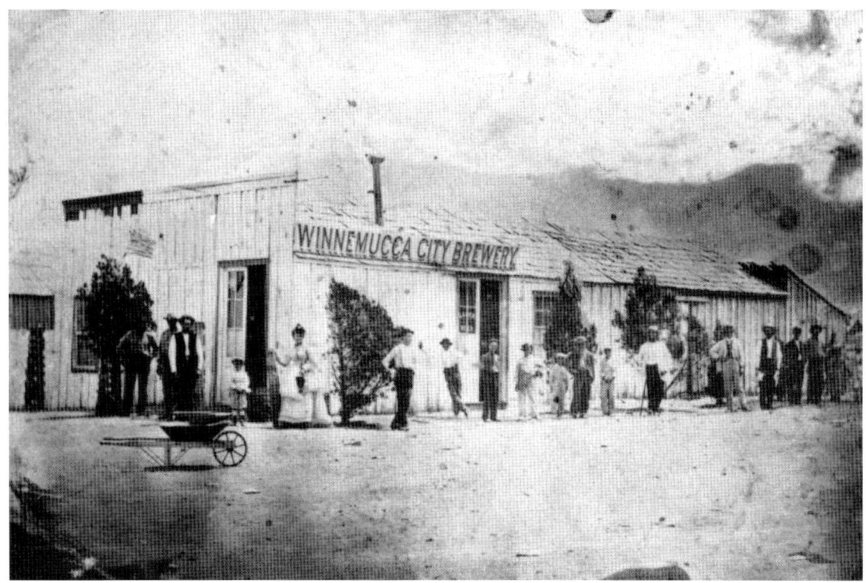

Winnemuca City Brewery was an early Nevada brewery, one of two in the mining town of Winnemuca. *Courtesy Nevada Historical Society.*

In Pioche, the Highland Brewery Depot sold cold lunches, including "German sausage, Holland herrings, pigs' feet, sheep's tongue, caviar and anchovies." Pioche was also home to the Meadow Valley Brewery.

Breweries were a sign of permanency for the population, as Robert Joe Stout alluded to in the *Nevadan Today* in 1988: "A mining camp was temporary until it boasted a brewery." Stout quoted Nevada prospector John Hoffman as saying, "Some batches were so bitter they'd roll your tongue down your throat and jam your ears together. But rinsed through the mouth with a little chaw, it had the kick of a blacksmith's hammer." Hoffman also was reported to suggest the consumers weren't likely to complain of a poor-quality beer; they were simply happy to be drinking.

Another source quoted in Stout's piece, Walter Weisz, suggested the beer was of excellent quality, essentially because Germans made it. The beer was likely thick and viscous, with a dark, cloudy appearance.

Beer served wasn't restricted to products brewed within the Silver State. Along with imports from the East Coast and Europe, breweries in other western states and territories took advantage of the surging population in Nevada.

RENO

The railroad brought the rise of Reno, and it soon became a competitor as the center of Nevada with Virginia City. Its first brewery, opened in 1868, was Reno Brewery by German immigrant Frederick Hertlein. The Washoe Brewery popped up in 1870, led by John George Becker and Charles Knust. A man by the name of William Hoffman seemed to like purchasing breweries, as he bought Reno Brewery's building in 1873. It burned down soon thereafter, as did Washoe Brewery.

Henry Riter was running his Elite Brewery at the Washoe Brewery building by the 1890s, making Elite Steam Beer, one of the prominent beers at the time in northern Nevada. Born in 1863 in Germany, Riter made his way at sixteen to California, where he became a butcher. A few years later, in 1884, he traveled to Reno, setting up the Elite Saloon, which was said to attract the most prominent people of Reno, according to Thomas Wren's *A History of the State of Nevada: Its Resources and People*.

In 1895, Riter purchased the Washoe Brewery from Hoffman, renaming it Riters Elite Brewery and making steam beer and porter. According to Wren, demand for Elite's beer was equal to the brewery's capacity. Steam beer is made with lager yeast fermented at the warmer temperatures normally used for ale yeasts. It was made this way due to a lack of refrigeration and cool temperatures, and some sources point to its invention in Nevada (certainly a disputed fact). Anchor Brewing Company maintains the tradition of making the style to this day. It trademarked the term in 1981 but makes it in a modern and presumably better quality.

Riter also owned Bowers Mansion, twenty miles south of Reno on the Virginia and Truckee Railroad, which he turned into a resort for the residents of Reno. Its seventy-five acres had hot and cold springs, along with two large swimming ponds. He was married to Lillian Dixon in 1888 and had an extensive circle of friends in Reno, Wren wrote. The historian also noted that Riter voted Democratic and was a member of the Knights of Pythias and Fraternal Order of Eagles.

A 1987 article chronicling Riter's life as thanks for the Bowers Mansion in the *Reno Gazette-Journal* reported that Riter was best known for the mansion. Along with the brewery, mansion and several saloons, Riter also started a reading room in Reno in 1901, a time when there was no public library, providing the city with current newspapers, national magazines and literature. He also owned parts of a nearby iron mine and power plant on the Truckee River and served as vice president of the Nevada Fire Insurance Company.

To help with the quality of his beer, he worked with Nevada farmers to grow a better grain for malt, according to the *Gazette-Journal* piece. His was a "prosperous institution" in 1904, when the *Gazette-Journal* reported it "a busy place nowadays" and also stated that fellow brewmaster Max Stenz in Goldfield was churning out "splendid quality of beer and porter" at Goldfield Brewery that was growing in popularity in both Reno and California.

Riter sold the brewery in 1904 to the startup Reno Brewing Company but stayed on in an official capacity for another thirteen years. He spent much of his time focused on the Bowers Mansion, which he purchased in 1903.

TRUCKEE

While Truckee is technically in California, Nevada was greatly served by Boca Brewing from that town. As the California gold rush took hold in 1849, breweries were popping up in the state to satisfy the new residents.

Many such breweries brewed their beers in seventy-two hours to help satisfy demand, leading to likely less-than-tasty beers of not very high potency.

According to the *Truckee Sun*, most of the hops and barley came from Sacramento and Napa Valleys, and many reports from early Nevada breweries suggested the same. In 1870, there were more than 155 breweries in California making more than 120,000 barrels of beer.

Truckee had a few small-batch brewers, including Truckee Brewing Company, St. Louis Brewery and Paul Menk Brewery & Saloon, according to the *Truckee Sun*, but in 1875, Boca Brewing Company opened a $100,000 facility six miles east of Truckee—the most expensive facility at the time west of the Mississippi River.

The area was excellent for "growing" ice, with long, cold winters with little precipitation. The Boca Mill and Ice Company was able to supply much of California with ice for boxcars so the fruits and vegetables grown in the state could be shipped east. With the ice accessible nearby, Boca Brewing opened and began producing thirty thousand barrels of lager a year. It was the first brewery to produce lager in California, and it won an award at the 1883 Paris World's Fair. Its location on the transcontinental railroad provided easy distribution across a wide swath of the United States, mostly on the Pacific coast. The beer was also sent to Mexico, Central and South America, Hawaii, China and Japan, according to the *Industries of San Francisco*.

Tourists to Truckee could visit the brewery, with its one-hundred-barrel brewhouse and a tank farm of twenty-five sixty-barrel fermenters. The tour of the facility finished with a glass of beer and a stop in the facility's three cellars, which all held at least fifty fifty-barrel casks of beer resting under twelve feet of ice for at least five months before they were packaged.

Despite its promising start, Boca Brewing wasn't long for the world. In 1893, the brewery caught fire and burned to the ground. The twelve-foot layer of ice saved many of the casks of beer in the cellars, but Internal Revenue collector W.L. Cole ordered them destroyed in his investigation, as they didn't have federal excise tax stamps. They were dumped into the Truckee River, creating a foaming mess. "A mournful assemblage of Boacites stood on the river's bank and with tearful eyes watched the sorrowful waste of the delicious beverage," the *Truckee Republican* stated.

The advent of mechanical refrigeration rendered the advantage of a nearby ice plant useless, and the location in the mountains actually further hurt the potential of a resurrection.

Nearly 120 years later, San Francisco's Anchor Brewing Company brewed up a re-creation of Boca's lager as the first of its Zymaster series of beers.

It was brewed with two-row barley, mountain water and Cluster hops, likely similar to the hop strain used in the 1800s. The recipe was meant to be maltier and hoppier than most standard lagers on the market today, as many on the market pre-Prohibition were. The Zymaster beer was a success, and Anchor continues to offer the beer as part of its year-round lineup. It is now known as California Lager.

Boca at the time was a small town but ballooned to 2,500 residents at its height, 80 of whom were employed by the brewery. Today, Boca is a ghost town.

Las Vegas

While it is the true hub of modern Nevada, Las Vegas was barely a circle on the map even into the early 1900s. Founded as a city in 1905 and incorporated in 1911, early Las Vegas lacked a brewery and instead was captured by Los Angeles's Maier and Zobelein Brewing Company with a bottling works as early as 1905.

PART II

EARLY BREWING POWERS

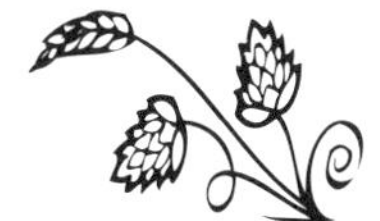

CHAPTER 4

CARSON BREWING COMPANY

While the slogan "Famous as the Lake" took years to develop for Carson Brewing Company and its Tahoe Beer brand, the brewery can lay claim to being the first and longest operating—unless Great Basin Brewing Company keeps chugging—in Nevada.

John Wagner and Jacob Klein established the brewery in 1860 on the corner of Second Street between Minnesota and Division Streets in Carson City. When production started at Carson Brewing, Nevada was still part of the Utah Territory, a year from becoming its own territory.

The original brewery was built with limestone from Curry's Hot Springs and was twenty feet wide by forty feet long, with twenty-inch-thick walls. The first brew kettle was seven barrels, and the brewery produced ninety barrels of steam beer in its first month, with all ninety being sold, according to *History of the Carson Brewing Company*.

As Carson City grew in 1865, Carson Brewing expanded into a two-story building that is still standing today as a National Historic Landmark on West King and South Division Streets. The new brewery was built with handmade bricks. The bar and offices were on the east side of the first floor, while Klein and Wagner worked with Carson Lodge to buy or rent the second story of the building and charged $100 rent. The lodge was housed on the second floor until 1919.

The bar, a big mahogany piece, was in operation from the second building's opening to the brewery's closure in 1948. Walls were lined with

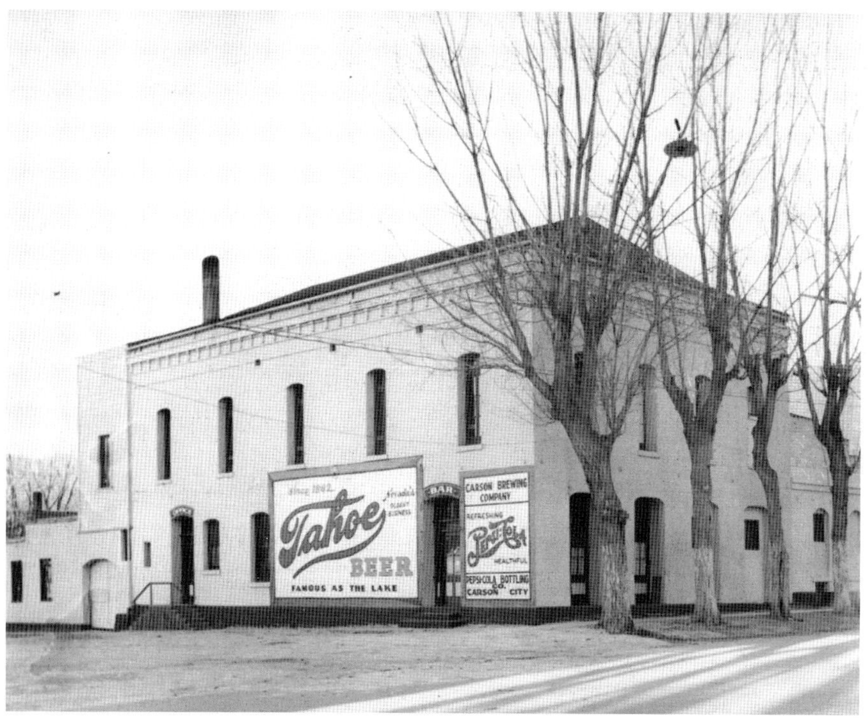

Carson Brewing Company's building in Carson City. The brewery was open from 1862 to 1947, serving up Tahoe Beer, "Famous as the Lake." *Courtesy Nevada Historical Society.*

cabinets, pictures and animal heads. Ore from the Comstock Lode was on display to showcase the reasons northern Nevada was so important. The brewery's museum also was home to the pistol of Sam Brown, described in the brewery's history as one of "the most ruthless killers to the wild West." When the brewery closed, the extensive collection housed in the barroom was donated to the Nevada State Museum in Carson City, housed in the old mint, which operated from 1870 to 1893.

While in operation, the bar was a gathering point for townspeople and served "Dutch lunches" of cold cuts, cheese, pretzels, crackers, potato chips, olives and pickles. The bar was similar to a German beer garden, with no music or singing allowed, and patrons enjoyed chicken dinners. Locals would also "rush the growler" and fill containers brought to the brewery with beer from the drafts.

On one Nevada Day, the brewery served twenty-one half barrels—more than 661 gallons—of beer to more than one thousand customers, according to *History of the Carson Brewing Company*.

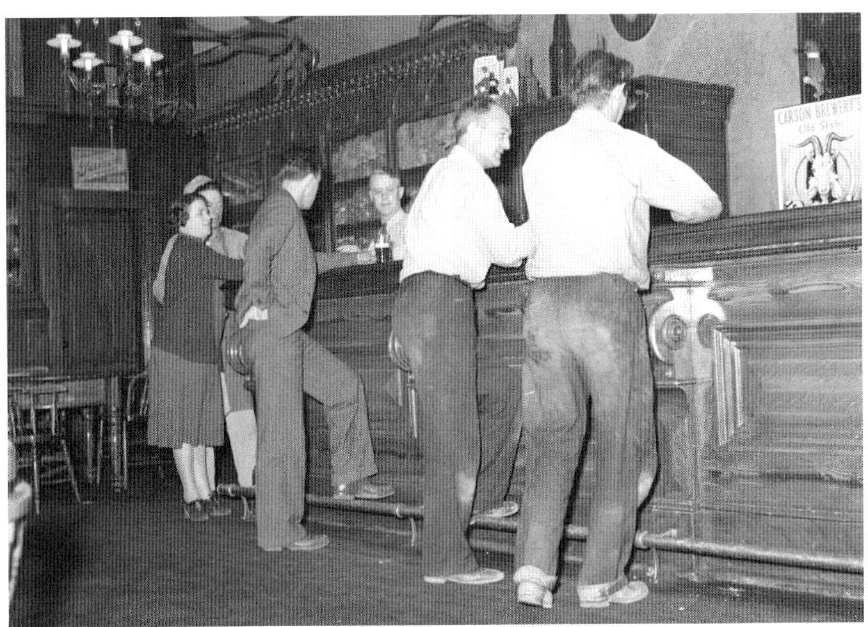

Patrons drink beers at the bar of Carson Brewing Company in 1940. *Courtesy Library of Congress.*

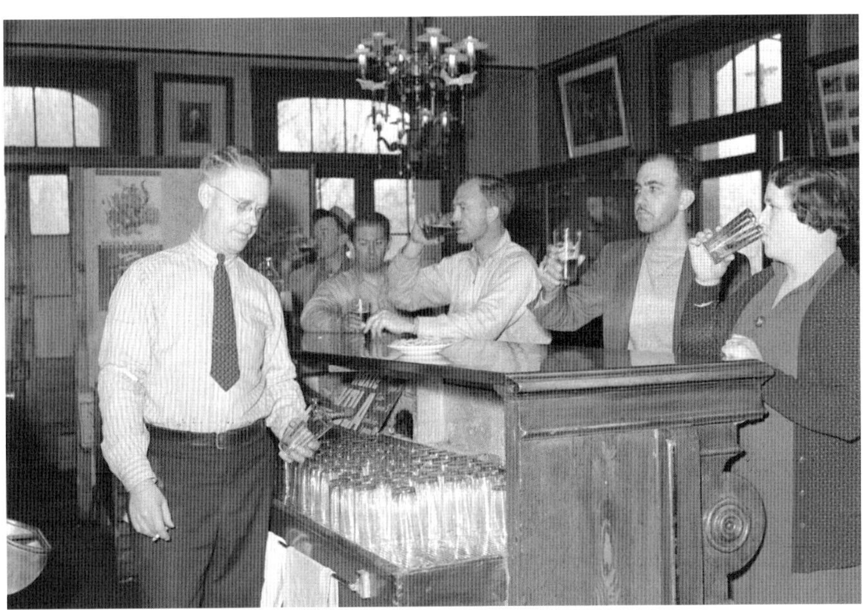

A bartender serves up beers at the Carson Brewing Company's bar in 1940. *Courtesy Library of Congress.*

Jacob Klein

Arnold Millard, the last owner of Carson Brewing when it closed in 1948 and the author of *History of the Carson Brewing Company*, went to great lengths to describe Jacob Klein as the true founder of the brewery in the business's definitive history.

Klein was born in 1831 in Alsace, France, where he took up baking as his trade. At nineteen, Klein departed for the United States, working in New York and Philadelphia before venturing in 1853 to San Francisco, where he made several thousand dollars mining in Placer County before promptly losing it, according to an 1883 manuscript. "Then I went into business of bakery, lodging house and saloon business," he wrote.

On April 18, 1860, he made his way through seven days of snow to get to Carson City. He described his entry into the brewing business with Wagner and another gentleman by the last name of Berhauser. When he arrived in Carson City, Klein wrote that there were only thirty or forty homes. Klein built a two-story house on South Division and West Second Streets, near the brewery.

Although it was small in size, Carson City apparently wasn't without drama. Klein wrote of an early court case in the city that saw a German woman kill a Spaniard. "I think the trouble grew out of a jealousy on his part," Klein wrote. "He was living in her house. He slandered her. A lawsuit arose about it in which the woman was a witness. Then she shot him. The Spaniard jumped about five feet high and then fell down dead. She was indicted for the murder, tried and acquitted by the jury in the court room where she had killed the deceased."

While much of recorded history suggests the West wasn't as wild as popular culture might lead its consumers to believe, Klein did write that Carson City had its wild side. "There was a pretty rough state of society in Carson City at that time," he wrote. "Two or three men were killed every six months. There were but few women here. Shooting affairs were of frequent occurrence. The town was infected with rough characters."

He would go on to describe several murders in 1862, but much of his recollections were on the way of life in the nineteenth-century mining town. He detailed the churches, which went up in this order: Catholic, Presbyterian, Methodist and Episcopal.

"It cost fifty cents to get a shirt washing here in 1860; the same price for shaving. Hair cutting was a dollar," Klein wrote. "Board at the hotels in 1860 cost about ten dollars a week, but people hardly got anything to eat. Transient customers paid a dollar a meal."

Wagner sold his shares of the brewery to Klein in 1879, which was also a tragic year for the brewery. A twenty-nine-year-old employee of Carson Brewing, Frank Nuss, fell into the brew kettle and burned to death.

Klein sold the brewery in 1888 to James Raycraft, a local stable owner.

Steam Beer and Production Process

From its founding, Carson Brewing was a steam beer producer. Millard went to great detail in describing the early process of making beer at the small brewery, starting with a scientific explanation of how malt was made, which the brewery did itself, "allowing the barley to soften in water and germinate. The enzyme diastase, developed during the germination process, catalyzed the hydrolysis of starch to the sugar maltose. (In simple language, the starch was turned into a sugar.) At this stage it was put into a wood-fired kiln and dried. The color of the beer depended on how long the malt was cooked."

Klein wrote that they paid ten cents per pound for freight of barley.

In the early days of the brewery, the brew kettle sat above a fireplace powered by wood. After the malt and hops were boiled in the brew kettle to create the pre-fermented wort, it was "drawn off into a 'ship.' The ship was a shallow metal tray sufficiently large to hold the brew. Metal tubs called 'floaters' were filled with ice to cool down the beer."

Once cooled, the beer was put into barrels and topped off with brewer's yeast to naturally carbonate the beer. The brewer's yeast was brought in every spring from Rainier Brewing Company in San Francisco; the brewery ceased operation during the winter and harvested in the cellar for brewing. Doctors would prescribe the yeast for some patients, and the brewery supplied it without charge.

In its first year of operation, Carson Brewing made more than five hundred barrels of beer, which required that it pay $100 for a federal brewing license and a $1-per-barrel tax, per a bill passed in Congress during the Civil War meant to help pay for the Union's war efforts.

MAX STENZ

James Raycraft, Frank Golden and F.A. Schultz incorporated Carson Brewing in 1900 and operated it for another ten years before selling the business to Max Stenz for $10,000, with a $4,500 loan from Father Gartland.

Stenz was urged to buy the brewery by his brother-in-law Fritz Hagmeyer, who was Carson Brewing's brewmaster at the time. Hagmeyer was the brewmaster from 1906 until 1912, eventually coming back in 1927 and working until he retired at sixty-five in 1943.

Stenz was born in Munich, Germany, in 1856 and made his way to America after serving in the German army. According to Millard's history, Stenz threw his German papers into the ocean and proclaimed he'd become an American citizen. He worked in the lumber mills of the Michigan forests, where his first wife and two children died during a scarlet fever epidemic. This tragedy sent him on a vaudeville tour, with which he yodeled.

In San Francisco, Stenz settled for a new life, marrying Agatha Willoth in 1882, with whom he had three more children, Frank, Max and Alma.

Stenz started his new career in breweries, first at San Jose Brewery before the family moved to Strawberry City outside Sacramento, where Stenz worked for Rhustaller's Brewery. Stenz eventually made a move to Goldfield, Nevada, where he helped start Goldfield Brewery in 1904 before selling his half in 1906 for $25,000. He then partnered with three other men to start Santa Cruz Brewing in Santa Cruz, California, before selling his stock in 1909, following which he made his way to Carson City at the suggestion of Hagmeyer.

Early in Stenz's operation, Carson continued to produce steam beer but also bought bottled beer from Santa Cruz Brewery, where his son Frank was the brewmaster, and distributed it around town.

Three years into his endeavor, Stenz sold some of his stock for capital for a production change. He wanted to make lager, ice, soft drinks and mineral water. A variety of investors purchased the stock, including hotel owner Wils Brougher, grocer Ed "Nevada Boy" Walsh, barber Ned Fothergill, cooper Frank Stupka, undertaker George Kitzmeyer, rancher Pete Heitman, barber J.B. Vierra, brewer John Krick, brewmaster Henry Kilian and rancher J.J. McEwen. Prior to the purchase, McEwen had harvested ice from his land in the winter for the brewery, but with the transaction, the brewery took over the business.

With the new investments, Carson Brewing built several new rooms and a building to house new equipment and extra storage, according to Millard.

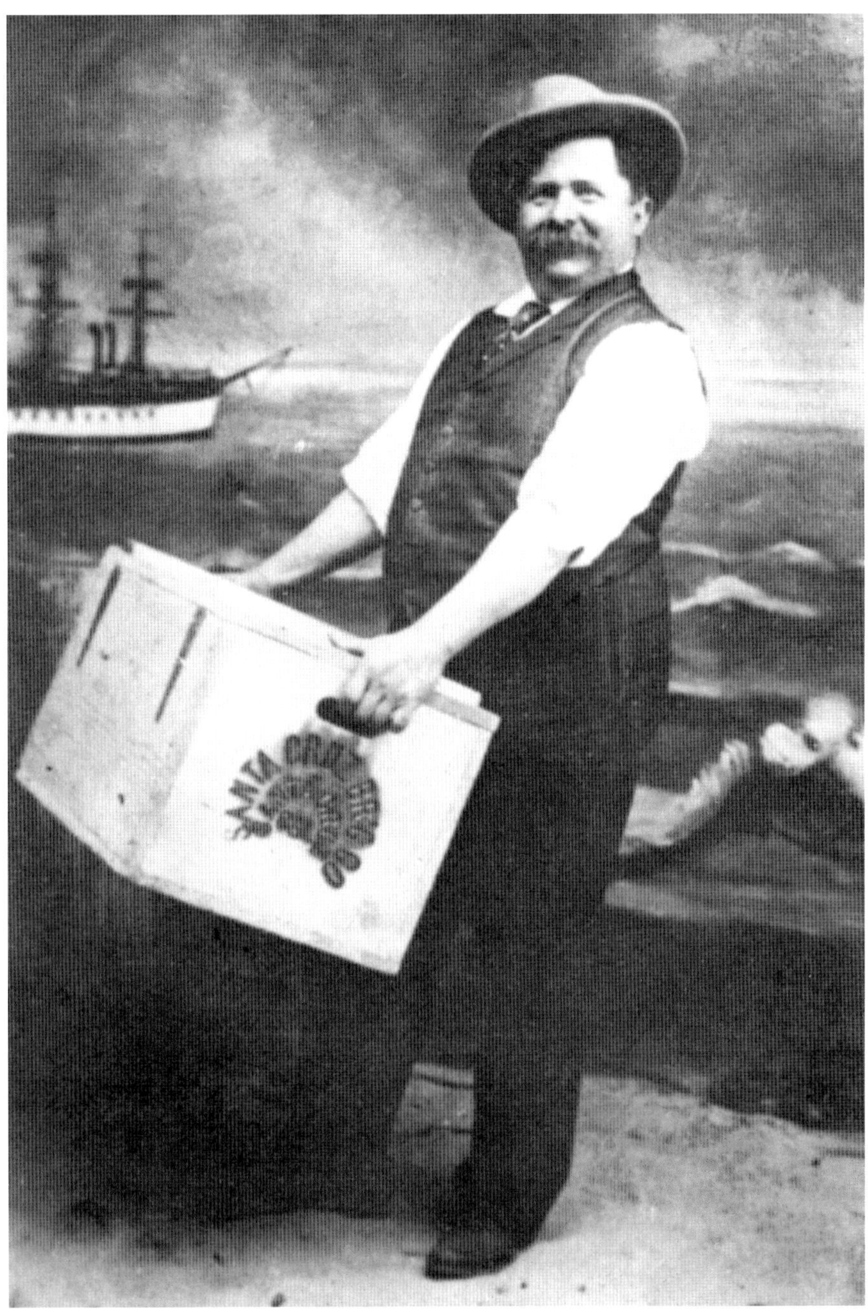

Max Stenz holds a case of beer. *Author's collection.*

The brewery also bought a twenty-ton Vulcan ice machine with a capacity to make five tons of ice daily, which was used to cool the operation and also delivered to local residents and businesses. Additionally, a forty-horsepower steam boiler was transitioned from wood to oil powered.

It was with these additions that Stenz converted Carson Brewing from producing steam beer to true lager beers, releasing Tahoe Beer and promoting the brew with the tagline "Famous as the Lake."

Lager

When brewing the lager, the brewery used sixteen sacks of malt, five sacks of rice and twenty pounds of hops to produce 1,600 gallons of beer per batch.

Milled malt was added to the mash tun, which housed a rotating agitator to stir the liquid, before rice that had been boiling in a separate pot was dumped into the kettle. The cooked liquid was drawn off into the brew kettle and boiled for five hours, and in the last twenty minutes, hops were added to the liquid.

The wort was then cooled to thirty-eight degrees through a Budlet Cooler, a series of two-inch refrigerated pipes standing seven feet tall and thirty feet in length. After the lengthy cooling period, the beer was poured into open wooden fermenters in the cellar, where the brewer's yeast was added and allowed to ferment for five days. As the yeast settled out, the beer was transferred to larger upright tanks, each holding several thousand gallons, and aged for six or more weeks before being filtered, carbonated and packaged in barrels or bottles.

Along with the light lager, Carson Brewing also brewed a bock beer, a darker and heavier lager or, as Millard called it, "one of the finest beers that was ever brewed."

Bottling was a laborious effort in the early twentieth century. After running through a bottle washer, the bottles were loaded into a twelve-spout hand-operated filler and then onto a stand where they were capped and loaded onto a twenty-four-bottle metal tray, which was then stacked into an eighty-tray pasteurizer that steam-heated water to 140 degrees for thirty minutes.

Carson Brewing installed a belt-driven, two-headed bottling machine for soft drinks that could bottle up to one hundred cases per day. The brewery also bottled mineral water from the Carson Hot Springs, brought by

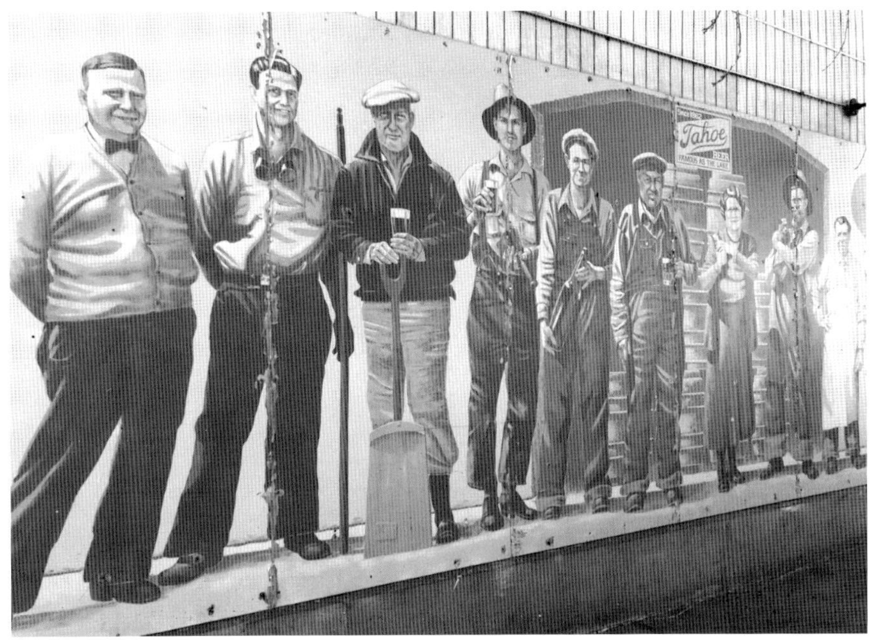

A mural of various Carson Brewing Company employees is painted on the modern façade of Carson Brewing Company's building. *Photo by Pat Evans.*

metal tank truck, cooled and bottled as "a very fine club soda," according to Millard.

Following the business's expansion and transformation to a lager brewery making Tahoe Beer, the company set up distribution outlets in Yerington, Fallon and Lovelock. Carson Brewing also sent beer and mineral water by refrigerated railcar to Reno. Deliveries were made in Dayton, Virginia City and the surrounding Carson Valley by an REO stake body truck, which Millard wrote was only the second truck purchased in Nevada. A Ford Model T truck was also purchased as a second truck for delivery across Carson of beer, soft drinks and ice. A Model T roadster was purchased for the brewery's salesperson, Max Stenz Jr.

PROHIBITION

As Prohibition settled on Nevada and the rest of the United States following the passage of the Volstead Act on January 21, 1918, Carson Brewing shareholders panicked, and Stenz was forced to buy back their stock, dollar for dollar, at the original price.

Kilian, who had been the brewmaster, resigned in 1918, seeing no future in the business, and was replaced by Gus Byer, who remained in the position until 1927. The brewery never stopped making beer; it just began brewing it at 2 percent, aging it and boiling it again to thin out the alcohol to the legal .5 percent near-beer level. The government allowed breweries to keep beer in bonded areas at the pre-Prohibition strength before removing alcohol and packaging it. Most breweries tried to do this with expensive distilling equipment, saving the alcohol and selling it to legal users. Carson Brewing, however, resorted to boiling, which ultimately saved countless amounts of money.

According to Millard, the locals loved the beer, and the brewery made money in a time when breweries across the country shuttered. Millard did write, however, that offers were made for the brewery to make illegal beer, with one family friend offering $10,000. Millard remained dutiful to the law.

In the midst of the dry era, in 1926, Stenz turned the brewery's day-to-day management over to his son-in-law Arnold Millard, who eventually would write the comprehensive history of the business in 1980.

Max Stenz Sr. died in 1929, and Millard was voted by family members as the president and general manager of the company.

ARNOLD MILLARD

Such a detailed history of Carson Brewing Company, written long after the business shuttered, is possible because of Millard's dedication to preserving its story.

Millard grew up in Carson City and remembered the days when he would go to a saloon with his father, who would buy a five-cent beer and get a free lunch, complete with ham, salami, boiled eggs, cheese, pickles, olives, pretzels, crackers and rye bread. Most bars did the same, and following Max Stenz's purchase of Carson Brewing, the brewery soon offered German potato salad, pickled herring, bologna, pretzels, Swiss cheese and rye bread on Sundays and holidays.

Millard had intimate knowledge of the Carson brewery, as he married Stenz's daughter, Alma, in 1921, when she was a bookkeeper at the brewery, a role she took over following her graduation from Oakland's Heald's Business

College. At the time of the marriage, Millard was working for Standard Oil Company, and Alma left the brewery. The pair returned when Max Stenz Jr. and his wife, Rose, left Carson Brewing to start their own business in California in 1925. The eldest Stenz persuaded Millard and Alma to join Carson Brewing Company with a hefty amount of stock.

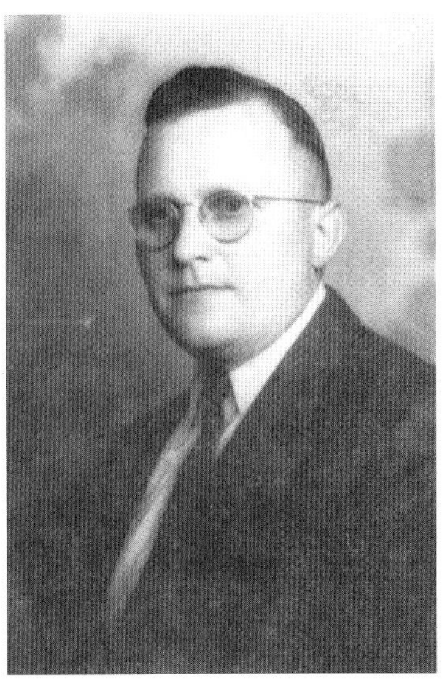

An early portrait of Arnold Millard, a longtime owner of Carson Brewing Company. *Author's collection.*

All was well until the perfect storm of bootleggers cutting into profits and the stock market crash of October 24, 1929. Millard wrote at that time it was necessary to diversify the business.

The brewery bought a wood and coal yard and a horse stable in 1930. The business sold fifty-four cars of wood and sixty thousand gallons of fuel in 1931, according to Millard's history. Prior to repeal, the government gave breweries permission to sell unfermented wort to consumers in 1932, which Carson Brewing did in five-gallon cans. Customers could buy the cans, add yeast and ferment their own brews.

Knowing repeal was on the horizon, Millard said the business made the decision to remodel and update the business to be better equipped to capitalize on the renewed industry. Millard stretched the company's "good credit" to buy a new steel hot water tank, grain elevators, a mash tank, a steam boiler, a malt mill and two ice machines. Carson Brewing also installed a new bottling system, increasing capacity from 100 cases a day to 750 cases.

Following the legalization of beer in 1933, the company was shuttered and used capital from the sale of the wood and coal yard to bolster the operation. Once beer was legalized, Millard wrote, the orders poured in, and it took six weeks for the brewery to catch up.

Tahoe Beer was sent all over the Reno-Tahoe area in both Nevada and California, but Millard said competition with the growing national brewing powers, namely Schlitz and Anheuser-Busch, was a struggle. "Business remained good for some time, but we were only a little brewery fighting the giants of the industry," Millard wrote. "Competition was keen, prices were cut. Some large breweries even furnished bars, backbars, ice bees, beer boxes, etc. to get business," a tactic still used in Nevada to this day.

CARSON BREWING'S DOWNFALL

There was little that could be done when World War II struck the globe. Rationing hit the United States hard. Carson Brewing's usage of malt, bottle caps and sugar was cut by 80 percent because of the government program. A decade after the end of one significant American historical event signaling the end of many U.S. breweries, rationing would cause another twenty-six to go out of business. Realizing a major issue affecting the industry, a label maker in Chicago started the Small Breweries Committee and lobbied the government to increase rations for breweries. This worked for malt but did not include the bottle cap crowns or sugar.

While Carson Brewing tried to stay afloat, the business bought hundreds of gallons of syrups to make different soft drinks and used extra malt. With the extra malt, Millard increased the brewery's fermentation capacity but was still limited by packaging with a lack of bottle crowns.

To work on this problem, crowns were collected from across the area and boiled to remove marketing labels and corks, leaving a question of how to reshape the caps for Carson's bottles. Millard rigged up a system with the help of a local railroad engineer that allowed for reshaping the caps, which allowed the brewery to meet its needs.

With this innovation, Carson Brewing survived the war's rationing. When former brewmaster Fritz Hagmeyer retired in 1943, the brewery was brewing and bottling six days a week.

In 1944, Reno's Harry Linnecke bought half the interest in the brewery. Two years later, the manager of the brewery's distributor in Reno, William Luce, bought the shares from Linnecke.

The beer was sent all over the West, including up to Seattle, thanks to Linnecke's salesmanship, Millard said. From Seattle, some went to Alaska, where it was featured in pictures in a 1947 *Collier's Magazine* piece about the Tenano River ice break.

Unfortunately, it was the period after World War II and the end of rationing that sent Carson Brewing to its end. The large breweries from east of the Rockies, including Schlitz and Budweiser, flooded the western markets, seeking a year-round market. Their mass production and large distribution infrastructure dating back even to before Prohibition dropped prices in the West, and Carson Brewing's costs no longer were justifiable.

The brewery was liquidated. The Pepsi Cola franchise was sold for $10,000, as were all of its beer, other beverages, bottles and redwood tanks. The brewery was officially closed on March 31, 1948.

The property was sold to Donald W. Reynolds in 1951, and the building was used as the *Nevada Appeal* newspaper offices and plant until another facility was built in town. The property was sold to the Carson City Arts Alliance, which still owns the building today.

MODERN COMEBACKS

Tahoe Beer made a comeback in the 1980s when an entrepreneur named Mark Lang sought to strike big with a nostalgic lager. While the craft beer movement was early, several businessmen across the country were set to try to bring back regional beers—the ones that weren't still in business. Lang relaunched Carson Brewing Company and was met with backlash, according to a 1985 *Reno Gazette-Journal* article.

The beer, however, wasn't being made in Nevada. It was brewed by Leinenkugel Brewing Company of Chippewa Falls, Wisconsin, before it was purchased by Miller Brewing Company. It should be noted there weren't many active breweries in 1985, with fewer than one hundred just a few years prior in 1979.

Leinenkugel archivists confirmed the brewery contract-brewed the Tahoe brand from 1982 to about 1984, brewing roughly 1,000 to 1,500 barrels of the brand. Lang purchased the bottles, crowns and labels; shipped them to Chippewa Falls for the brewing; and paid for freight, according to Leinenkugel representatives.

Lang bought the brand from the Millard family in 1982, with the intention of only selling the beer within fifty miles of Carson City. According to the article, despite being made in Wisconsin, it was a "quality beer," using 100 percent malted barley. Many of the beer makers at the time, including Budweiser and Miller, used adjuncts in their lagers like corn and rice.

Lang said in 1985 that he hoped to build a brewery with a capacity of 150,000 barrels annually, but the $13 million price tag he estimated was never accomplished. So his dreams of hiring 180 employees and attracting a million tourists a year were abandoned. He was ahead of his time.

"There hasn't been a small commercial brewery built in this country in 80 years," Lang said in 1985, seemingly unaware of a budding microbrewery industry. "We're not going to ask people to buy our beer because we're David against Goliath. We're going to ask them to buy it because we've got good product and we're proud of it."

Today, Tahoe Beer is sold by the Brewer's Cabinet in Reno. Three varieties of Tahoe Beer—Blonde, Pale Ale and Amber—join the business's lineup of outstanding modern beers. The blonde Tahoe Beer is a refreshing crisp take on a light golden ale, brewed with old-world hops from Germany and Czech Republic. While the blonde is more suitable for drinkers wary of heavy craft beers, the amber ale is used to help convert those drinkers with a tad more complexity by using toasty malts and Pacific Northwest hops. The pale ale is the Brewer's Cabinet's tribute to the great craft pale ales brewed in the recent past, as it's much more hop-forward and citrusy than any pale ales that might have been brewed prior to Prohibition.

CHAPTER 5

RENO BREWING COMPANY

Founded in 1903, Reno Brewing Company produced Sierra Beer until 1957, save for the years when beer production was forbidden during Prohibition. The brewery was housed in a large facility on East Fourth Street in Reno with a capacity of one million gallons of beer.

Reno Brewing was started by a trio of entrepreneurs who made their way to Nevada from Montana with beer mugs in their eyes. Peter Dohr, Jacob Hook and John Mauer all met in Butte, Montana, before making their way southwest.

Sam Post Davis wrote in his definitive *The History of Nevada* that Hook was born in Hesse-Darmstadt, Germany, in 1866 and learned to brew in his homeland before immigrating in 1885 to the United States, where he settled in Indianapolis, Indiana.

A 1939 *Nevada State Journal* article reported that Hook was first trained by his father and later graduated from Chicago's Wahl-Henius Institute of Fermentology in 1895. He spent eight years at an Indianapolis brewery before making his way to Cincinnati, Ohio, for two years. Eventually, he made his way to Rossland, British Columbia, where he built Lyon Brewery. Four years later, he traveled to Butte, where he worked for three years for Butte Brewing Company. Hook met Dohr at the Montana business.

According to Davis's history, Dohr was born in Appleton, Wisconsin, in 1874 and headed in 1898 to Montana, where he worked for four years. He moved to Reno in 1902, along with Hook and Mauer.

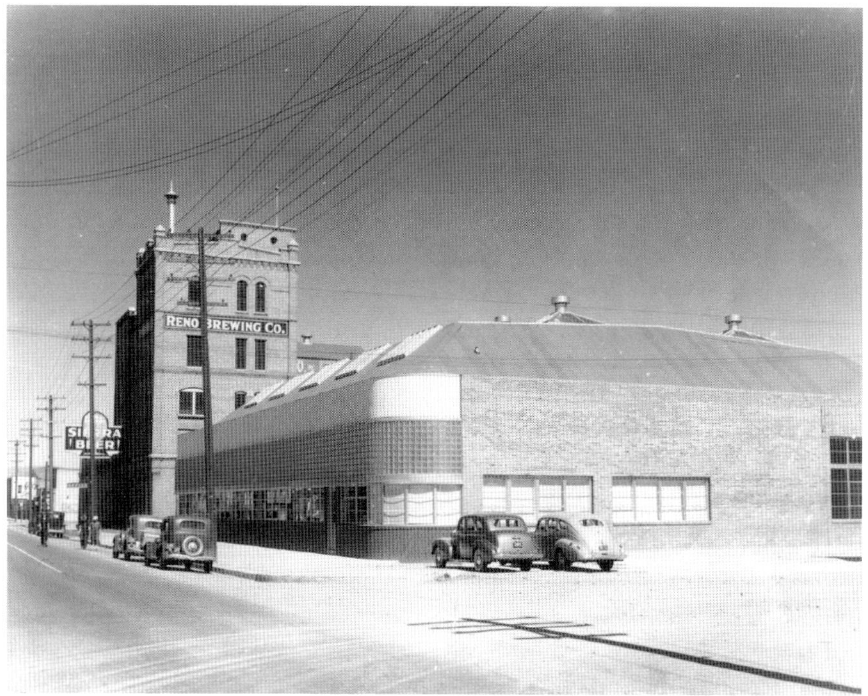

Reno Brewing Company's main building and icehouse. Reno Brewing was in operation from 1903 to 1958. *Courtesy Nevada Historical Society.*

Hook was the master brewer of Reno Brewing, which opened officially on July 24, 1903, with a public celebration with more than one thousand barrels of Sierra Malt Lager and a performance by the Reno Wheelmen's Band. Six months after the brewery's official incorporation in March 1904, Reno Brewing took over Riters Elite Brewery, with a new incorporation filed in September 1904. Early twentieth-century photos of Nevada saloons also had a fair amount of Milwaukee's Schlitz Brewing Company advertisements.

Reno was a sizable town at this time, and while Reno Brewing swallowed its main local competitor in Riters, a variety of other brewers were shipping beer to town and packaging it in bottling works, including the Rainier Bottling Works of Seattle Brewing and Malting Company and the John Wieland Bottling Works, which was the hub for San Francisco's lager giant John Wieland Brewery.

As the reputation of Reno Brewing spread and marketing of the products extended into Nevada's new mining camps, it embarked on the construction of a new six-story brick building, which would go on to house sixteen glass-enabled fermentation tanks with a capacity of 3,400 barrels of beer. Along with the enameled fermenters were wood storage tanks and fermenter for a total capacity of 8,000 barrels. With the newfound capacity, Reno Brewing added Malt Rose and Royal Lager to the beer lineup and cold storage depots in Yerington, Fallon and Lovelock, Nevada, and Truckee, California.

Distribution of Reno Brewing beers eventually reached some California and Oregon markets, as well as occasional shipments to Idaho and Utah, according to the *Henderson Home News*.

By 1910, demand had surged, and Reno Brewing expanded to a capacity of forty thousand barrels by 1916.

In a 1914 *Reno Gazette-Journal*, Reno Brewing Company's facilities were described as the "most modern in the west," and it was stated that the "scientific process yields fine product." The article then detailed the "gravity process," starting with malted barley on the fifth floor and working down the building until cellaring in the basement. Barley was kept in a three-story container at the top of the building and put through a mill, then passed through a magnet, which would collect any metals. In the brewing process in 1914, more than 5,800 pounds of malted barley, corn and hops were used to make 115 barrels of beer. Hops from California were used at the time.

The beer was fermented in seventeen 60-barrel tanks before being cellared in fourteen 140-barrel tanks, two 120-barrel tanks and two 90-barrel tanks. The tanks, at least many of them, were purchased from a New York manufacturer that lined steel tanks with glass enamel. Following a lengthy cellar time, the beer was stored in twelve 80-barrel and four 100-barrel tanks, from which the finished brew was packaged.

A 1916 *Nevada Newsletter* featured advertisements touting the beers of Reno Brewing Company. Sierra and Royal Beers were described as the "best part of the evening meal," as they allowed drinkers to "take a little journey in contentment."

"And when you take a little journey with Sierra or Royal Beer, you travel first-class, for no other beer can give you the same delight as the home brew," one of the advertisements read. A telephone number of 581 was listed, and the reader was told the ring "will bring a case promptly to your door."

Sierra Beer advertisements in papers during the early twentieth century featured Wild West wanted posters, with outlaws like Chinless Charlie, Filthy Dan, Hans Biersnatcher and Weepin' Willie. "Your reward is always ample in cool, refreshing Sierra Beer," they read.

George Johnson took over office management of Reno Brewing in 1907. Prior to his time in Reno, Johnson was born in Chicago in 1882 before heading to Cleveland, Ohio, where he became engrained in manufacturing. In 1905, he headed to Seattle, where he joined Seattle Brewing and Malting Company. Davis made note that Johnson was a Republican and a member of the Eagle lodge, as well as a successful pianist and composer.

Johnson helped lead Reno Brewing through Prohibition, during which the brewery produced near beer, soda water, seltzers, tonics and soft drinks, gliding through the more than a decade that ultimately spelled doom for so many of the nation's breweries.

The Dohr family reacquired the title of the brewery in 1943, with Ronald Dohr, Peter Dohr's son, becoming president shortly after a renovation and addition of a bottling house to the brewing facility. A full renovation of the facility was performed in 1948.

In 1950, the brewery had capacity for brewing forty-five thousand barrels a year and had a bottling line capable of ninety bottles per minute.

Sierra Beer at the time, according to the *Nevada State Journal*, was "as familiar as sagebrush to practically all the people in Nevada who live north of Clark and Lincoln counties," when it was the only brewery remaining in Nevada.

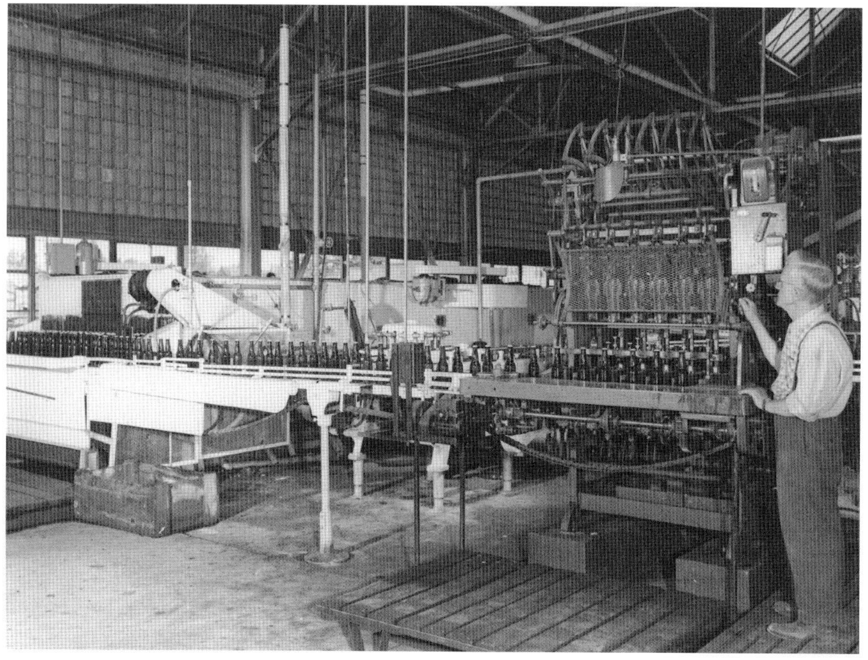

A Reno Brewing employee operates the company's bottling machine. *Courtesy Nevada Historical Society.*

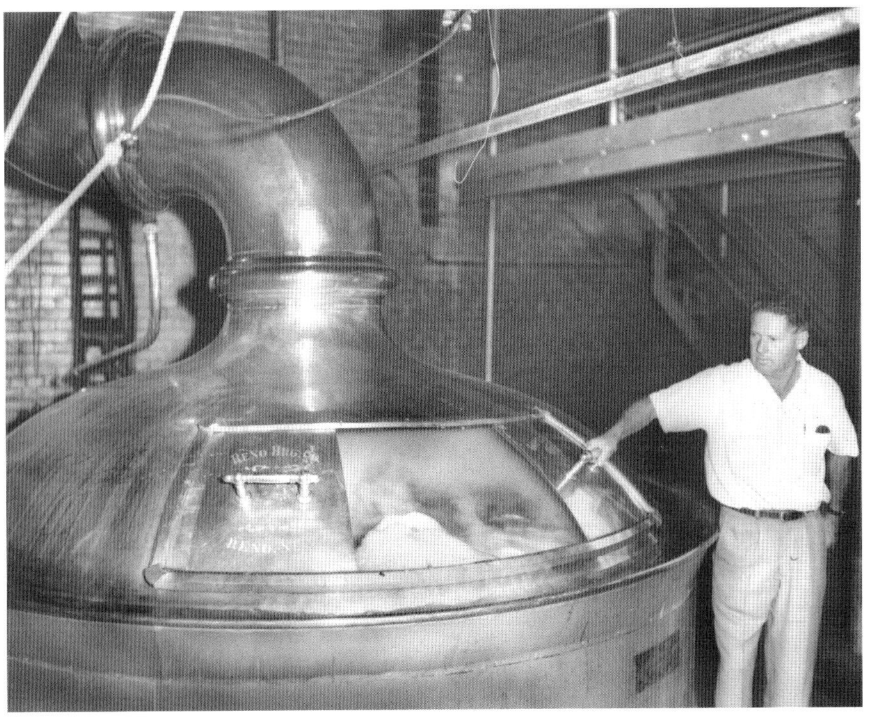

A Reno Brewing Company brewer watches over a batch of beer as it boils in the kettle. *Courtesy Nevada Historical Society.*

Sierra Beer, according to the in-depth *Nevada State Journal* piece, took more than four months to make. Corn from Kansas and California, malted barley from Wisconsin and hops from Washington and Oregon were used in the process. The corn made the beer lighter and "adds more nourishing qualities," while the hops "impart to the brew its special tangy flavor and the years provides the sparkle."

Brewing was performed at night in a mostly automated ten-hour process in a 120-barrel copper-topped brew kettle. Fermentation took ten days, and the beer was then cellared for a month, filtered and stored for another month. Following a second filtering, the beer was bottled and ready for shipment, mostly to the northern counties of Nevada but also to some adjoining counties in California. Shipping to lower Nevada was "impractical."

In the 1950 article, it mentioned a worker who had been with the company since 1904, Dan Drewitz. When he started, Drewitz delivered beer via horse-drawn wagon but transitioned into other roles as he and the company aged.

In 1952, the brewery released "handy, flat-top cans" for easy stacking that "fit neatly into fishing kits." The beer within the cans was guaranteed to be one of the longest-aged beers in Nevada and, therefore, "lighter and dryer."

Ronald Dohr took over full management of the brewery in 1953 after the retirement of Carl Fuetsch, before millionaire businessman LaVere Redfield purchased Reno Brewing in 1954. Because of the brewery's size, it was speculated that a California or eastern U.S. brewery might be interested in the site to produce for the Nevada market as the beer industry condensed nationwide. Redfield, as it turned out, purchased the brewery building to secure indebtedness, according to a 1954 article in the *Reno Gazette-Journal*. Dohr and Redfield came to an agreement to allow Dohr to remain in charge of the brewing operation within the facility, according to the *Gazette-Journal*. At the time, Sierra and One Sound State beers were Reno Brewing's flagships.

The brewery was returned to the Dohr family in 1957 but halted production the same year because of increasing pressures from the large, growing Midwest brewing conglomerates. Ronald Dohr died in 1973 at the age of sixty-nine.

The brewery was sold in auction in October 1958, according to the *Reno Gazette-Journal*. The article noted that "paper clips, typewriters, desks and miscellaneous items were the first to go" before explaining that the real estate and building were yet to go on sale. Items left to sell also included ice machines, bottling and canning equipment and trucks.

Fred Newburg, the San Francisco auctioneer in charge of the sale, told the newspaper that the brewery would cost $1.5 million to replace. The operation "lost money steadily in the years before operation was halted," the *Gazette-Journal* reported. "We don't expect to get that much," Newburg told the paper.

The highest bid for the facility went to Reno real estate investor Norman Blitz, who offered $190,000 for the bottling plant, $75,000 for the brewery building and $50,000 for the land between the brewery and the Southern Pacific Railroad, for a total of $315,000. Blitz's offer didn't stand, and the building ultimately ended up in the hands of Joe Hobson and the Frontier Land and Cattle Company.

The brewery building was torn down in 1959, but the bottling works building still stands as of 2018.

RENO BREWING'S STRANGE RESURGENCE

In the 1990s, a Reno Brewing brand relaunched in Nevada. In 1994, Kirk Ellern announced he planned to build a brewery called Reno Brewing in downtown Reno, but when plans fell through, he contracted Cold Springs Brewery in Minnesota to brew the company's Ponderosa Pale Ale. Cold Springs Brewery is a pre-Prohibition brewery, founded in 1874, still in operation today.

Later in 1994, Ellern told the *Reno Gazette-Journal* that he still planned to open a brewery in Truckee Meadows. By 1995, it became obvious to Ellern that he was fighting an uphill battle against distributors, which had lobbied in the 1991 brewpub law allowing the businesses to restrict them to redevelopment areas. Ellern found any suitable properties to be cost-prohibitive, as was the prospect of continuing to brew in Minnesota and ship it back, according to the *Gazette-Journal*.

Reno Brewing was one of the first Reno businesses to set up an online operation in 1994, according to a 1996 *Gazette-Journal* article about the surge in online business pages.

By 1996, Reno Brewing Company's Ponderosa Pale Ale and Wolf Pack Wheat Ale were in forty-one states, thanks to a partnership with a national distributor. The *Gazette-Journal* projected the brand would be in all fifty states by 1997.

Mentions of the company tapered off, and no records of its cessation are available.

CHAPTER 6

DRY TIMES

State prohibition took hold in Nevada in 1918, when the state's voters chose to go dry with 60 percent of them voting in favor of prohibition. The state ratified the Eighteenth Amendment on January 16, 1919, but had already started to follow the new law by December 17, 1918, along with President Woodrow Wilson's Wartime Prohibition.

In northern Nevada, where most of the state's residents still lived at the time, saloons closed in short order. In Las Vegas, the sheriff at the time, Sam Gay, waited until the holidays, with the warning, "I am going to enforce the prohibition law to the letter. Mr. Bootlegger, this is your first and final notice from me. Your next notice will be a warrant for your arrest. All drugstore clerks should read this notice." Gay had stopped drinking in 1915, when the six-foot, 260-pound sheriff drunkenly shot out the electric lights on Fremont Street.

With the Volstead Act enacted by Congress, Prohibition officially took effect on January 17, 1920.

Bootleggers found relative safe havens in Eldorado Canyon, Searchlight and Indian Springs. Much of the alcohol actually came to the Las Vegas area from the Arizona Strip, a lawless area because of the Grand Canyon and Nevada and Utah borders.

Nevada complicated the issue for itself when the state legislature decided to repeal the state law, meaning local law enforcement no longer had to enforce the issue. Despite some light regulations, saloons were open in Las Vegas. Federal agents, however, conducted regular raids in that city. Even

Las Vegas mayor Fred Hesse was arrested for running a still to make alcohol for bootlegger James Ferguson.

Las Vegas was so small in the 1920s that there were no federal buildings, and the nearest agents were located in Los Angeles, meaning the raids weren't regular. However, a raid in 1925 closed down at least nine establishments for a year on the city's Block 16, a row of saloons in Las Vegas's early city planning. A similar raid in 1928 led to the arrest of at least a dozen speakeasy and saloon owners who ultimately paid $4,800 in fines.

A planned visit by Secretary of the Interior Ray Lyon Wilbur and Commissioner of the Bureau of Reclamation Elwood Mead was slated for June 21, 1929, to determine if Las Vegas could be an ample home for the workers soon to call southern Nevada home for the Boulder Dam project. With the visit in mind, the Las Vegas City Council asked Police Chief Percy Nash to shut down and disguise saloons for their visit. Prior to the visit, a federal raid took place. It shut down nine stills and four breweries and collected more than 3,500 gallons of mash, 228 gallons of whiskey, 571 cases of beer and 470 gallons of other types of booze.

With the revelation that Las Vegas wasn't a clean city, the government decided to build Boulder City as a "federal reservation," a community covered by its own laws and free of drinking and gambling to provide a healthy and productive lifestyle for the workers building what would become the Hoover Dam.

Nevada had the highest opposition rate of Prohibition by 1930, according to a published poll by *Literary Digest*. It's likely because of this that the federal government placed a high priority on raids in Las Vegas. On January 9, 1931, twenty-three agents came to Las Vegas and arrested fifty-six people and seized four thousand bottles of booze and thirty thousand gallons of mash.

Upon repeal of Prohibition, and likely because of the lax environment by local police, it was found by Nevada federal judge Frank Norcross that the state had the best enforcement during the Noble Experiment.

RENO

In Reno, Henry Riter kept the Bowers Mansion bar flowing. Officially, he had turned the bar into a soda parlor, but for those with whom he had developed a trust, alcohol was freely served. Riter had a variety of side businesses running out of the mansion, including raising goldfish in one of his hot pools and starting the Reno Mineral Water Company, bottling water from the thermal springs on the property.

A *Reno Gazette-Journal* article in 1985 reported that federal agents had known of the activity but failed to prove it until an undercover agent was served a drink on May 8, 1922. Two more agents were served drinks on May 10 of the same year, and Riter and the bartender were arrested. More than two hundred gallons of wine and another "quantity of 'jackass brandy'" were discovered. Riter was sentenced to four months in jail for the federal offense in 1923.

The mansion was sold by Henry Riter and his wife, Edna, in 1946 to the Reno Women's Civic League. Riter died in 1949.

In downtown Reno, as construction began on the train depot in 1925, workers found soured champagne bottles in a cellar and began drinking them, according to an article in the *Reno Gazette-Journal*. Prohibition agents shortly showed up and smashed the bottles.

Reno's Douglas Alley was known as a "Wet Alley" or "Bottle Alley" and included many saloons like the Harrah's Plaza Tango, Wine House, National Club, Mecca Club, Reno Club, State Club, My Cellar and the Casino. Three were raided in succession in 1926.

Reno casino mogul James McKay was raided in what the *Sparks Tribune* called the "biggest rum raid ever," according to the *Gazette-Journal*. Federal agents from San Francisco took more than $75,000 worth of alcoholic products from McKay's house in 1923.

Prohibition's End

The nation repealed Prohibition on December 5, 1933, as the Twenty-First Amendment passed. While the amendment once again allowed the legal sale of alcoholic products, laws within the alcohol sector are still greatly influenced by the after-effects of the nation's dry spell.

In a July 1932 issue of the *Nevada State Journal*, a headline read, "Real Beer in 24 Hours, That's All the Time Needed by Reno Plant If Volstead Law Is Modified." Prior to repeal, Reno Brewing was producing a beer of less than 1 percent ABV, which didn't sell well. While manager Jacob Hook said production would start once repealed, he also said he had real beer stored for eight months, as near beer was made from real beer but with the alcohol evaporated. "First we make good beer," Hook said in December 1932. "Then we spoil it to make near-beer."

Once Volstead was repealed, they put the mature beer on the market.

"We will sell 20 times, no, 50 times more beer than we do this weak stuff," Hook told the paper in the July issue. "Maybe prohibition has taught everyone how to make their own home-brew. But when we show them how real beer tastes, they'll drop their home talent stuff and drink ours."

On April 6, 1933, it was reported by the *Nevada State Journal* that fifty-four establishments applied for beer licenses. Most of these locations would sell a glass of beer for ten cents. In total, the fifty-four applicants paid the city $1,325. In the same article, Reno Brewing was reported to have hundreds of barrels and cases ready for a 6:00 a.m. delivery on April 7, but residents could head straight to the brewery at midnight, "thereby getting a head start for their business, or for their own 1933 quota of suds."

Before Prohibition ended nationally in 1933, Nevada was well on its way to becoming a destination for much of America's vices. Despite a 1909 statewide criminalization of gaming, laws eased in licensed card rooms and other forms of gambling before gaming was fully legalized on March 19, 1931, with a law signed by Governor Fred Balzar. In 1930, Nevada had a population of 89,168 and was coming off a difficult decade in which there was even talk of taking statehood away from the Silver State.

In October 1937, Carson Brewing and Reno Brewing brewed a collective 1,652 barrels of beer, according to the *Reno Gazette-Journal*, the fourth lowest among all states and well behind New York's four breweries, which turned out 628,613 barrels in October.

Prohibition, sadly, was the end of the first great beer age of the United States. Although plenty of breweries were able to survive or start back up following the Noble Experiment, few were able to make it much beyond 1950, as the nation commoditized many products and several breweries—Schlitz, Anheuser-Busch and later Miller and Coors—were able to catapult to market dominance. While the roots of the current beer age were planted in 1965 when Fritz Maytag purchased San Francisco's Anchor Brewing, the late 1970s was a low point in the U.S. beer industry, with fewer than 80 breweries nationwide. It wasn't until 2015 that the U.S. brewing industry passed the 1873 pre-Prohibition high of 4,131 breweries in operation. In 2018, there are more than 6,500 breweries in operation, but Nevada is among the fewest in the nation (fewer than 45 in 2018) due to a variety of circumstances, including an industry focused on cheap beer, fine wine and pricey cocktails.

CASINO BOOM

The modern Nevada beer industry is inherently shaped by the past eighty years of gaming developments in Nevada. Without the dominance of gaming corporations, the state would look a whole lot different, and while the industry has held back local breweries by many accounts, without them the state would possibly not even exist.

A few years following Prohibition's repeal, William Fisk Harrah opened his first of many establishments in 1937 with a bingo parlor in Reno. Harrah's Entertainment grew into what is now Caesars Entertainment.

Mobster Bugsy Siegel opened the Flamingo Hotel on the Las Vegas Strip in 1946, just a few months before he was murdered. His entry into the development of the Flamingo was in an effort to rebrand himself as a legitimate businessperson after spending much of the 1930s helping supply illegal booze to the workers at the Hoover Dam.

By 1950, Nevada's population had neared 160,000. The ensuing decade included several notable events, such as the Tropicana and Riviera opening on the Strip and the creation of the Nevada State Gaming Commission. In another ten years, the population neared 285,000, with gaming revenues of $200.5 million and the original Caesars Palace opening. In 1970, the population was nearing 500,000, and the '70s ushered in the true tourism era of Nevada, as it became the number one industry.

The sports betting tax was also lowered in the 1970s, allowing for a boom in sportsbooks. Gaming tax revenues in Clark County surpassed $1 billion in 1977. The big business of casino tourism continued with the launch of the $750 million mega-resort the Mirage in 1989, welcoming a new era of Las Vegas and a continued influence on how the state's liquor business worked.

As the fastest-growing state in the Union for much of the 1980s, Nevada reached 1.2 million residents in 1990, with an economy dominated by twelve publicly owned companies. Twenty-one casinos made up 50 percent of the state's gaming revenue, which by 1993 surpassed $6 billion per year. The 1990s experienced a boom of some of the most famous Las Vegas resorts, including New York New York, Excalibur, Luxor, Treasure Island, MGM Grand, Monte Carlo, Bellagio, Paris, Venetian and Mandalay Bay. Over the course of the 1990s, the population nearly doubled, to 2 million people in 2000, and gaming revenues surpassed $10 billion annually by 2004 and $12.5 billion in 2006.

Throughout the first decade of the new millennium, major casino and hotel projects continued to shape how influential the industry is to the entertainment culture in Nevada. MGM Grand Inc. merged with Mirage Resorts Inc., which, in turn, merged a few years later with Mandalay Resort Group, ultimately rebranding as MGM Resorts International in 2010. MGM announced the CityCenter Project in 2009, a $7 billion project that would result in the construction of Vdara Hotel & Spa, Aria Resort & Casino and Mandarin Oriental. Harrah's Entertainment, meanwhile, purchased Caesars Entertainment. Other hotels to open included Wynn and Encore and the Palazzo. Cosmopolitan Hotel opened in 2010.

In 2013, MGM announced plans for an arena, a $375 million partnership with AEG, finished in 2016. T-Mobile Arena would soon be home to the National Hockey League's Vegas Golden Knights, the first major-league sports franchise in Las Vegas.

PART III

MODERN BEER

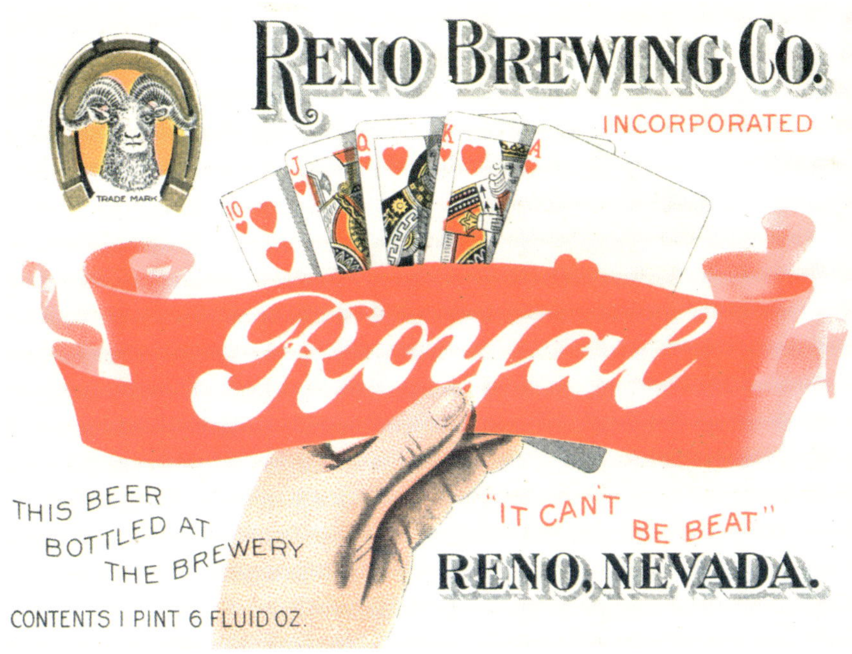

Above: A Royal beer label, brewed by Reno Brewing Company. Royal was one of the main brands brewed by the brewery, which operated from 1903 to 1957. *Author's collection.*

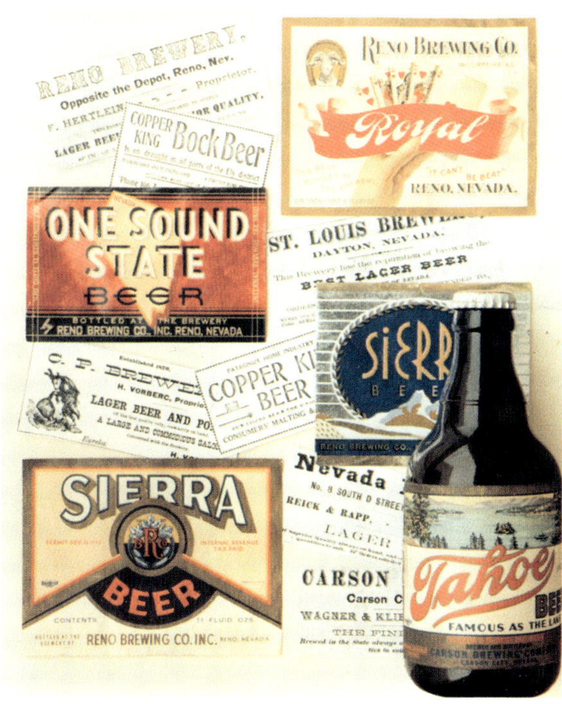

Left: The cover of *Brewed in Nevada*. Robert Nylen and Eric Moody pulled together this history of Nevada beer prior to any of the modern breweries. *Author's collection.*

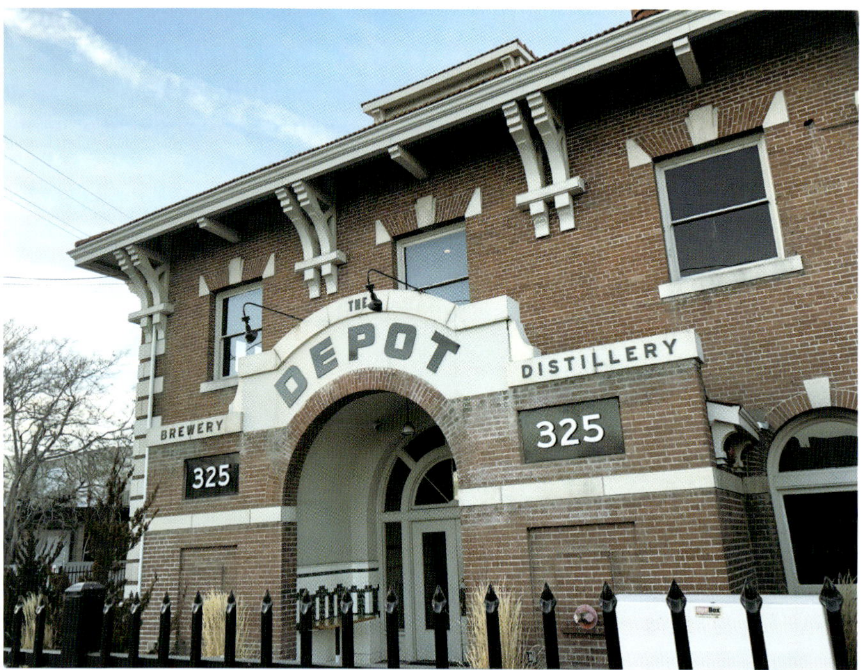

The Depot Craft Brewery Distillery is located on Fourth Street in Reno. The brewery is housed in a former train depot, built in 1910. *Photo by Pat Evans.*

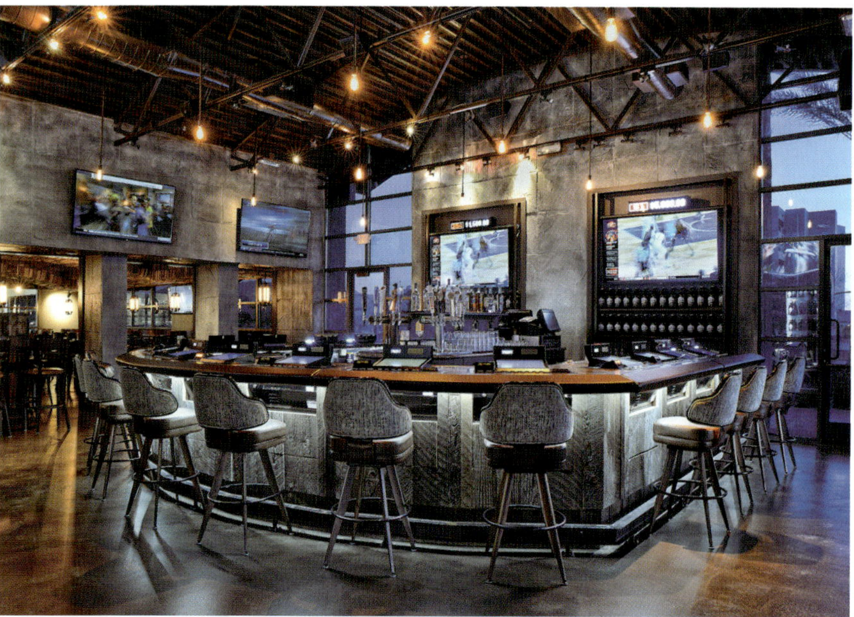

The interior of PT's Brewing Company, located in the original Tenaya Creek Brewery. There are more than fifty company pubs owned by PT's serving the beer brewed at this location. *Courtesy PT's Brewing Company.*

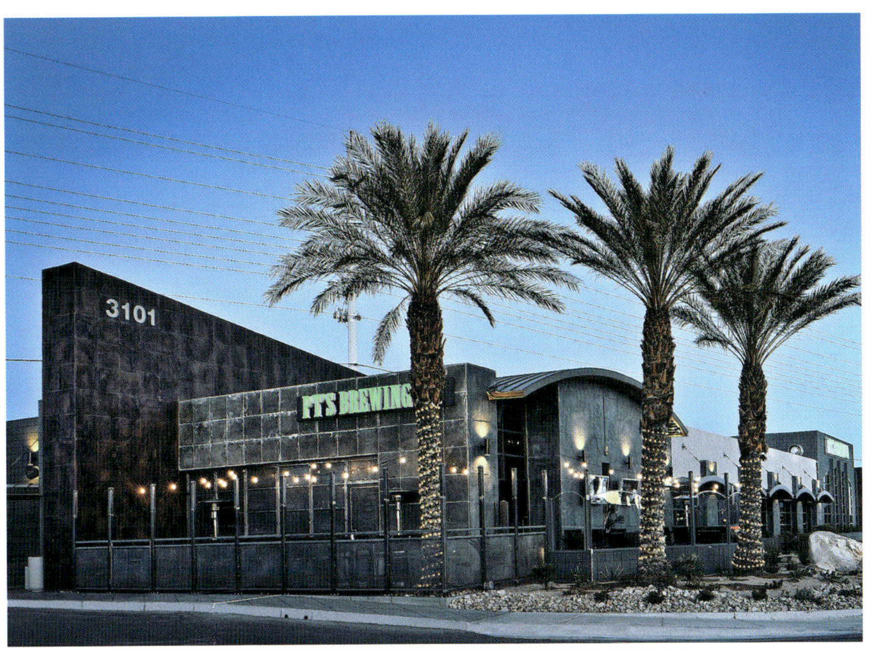

PT's Brewing Company opened in 2016 in the former Tenaya Creek Brewery after it moved downtown. Longtime Las Vegas brewer Dave Otto started as the brewmaster. *Courtesy PT's Brewing Company.*

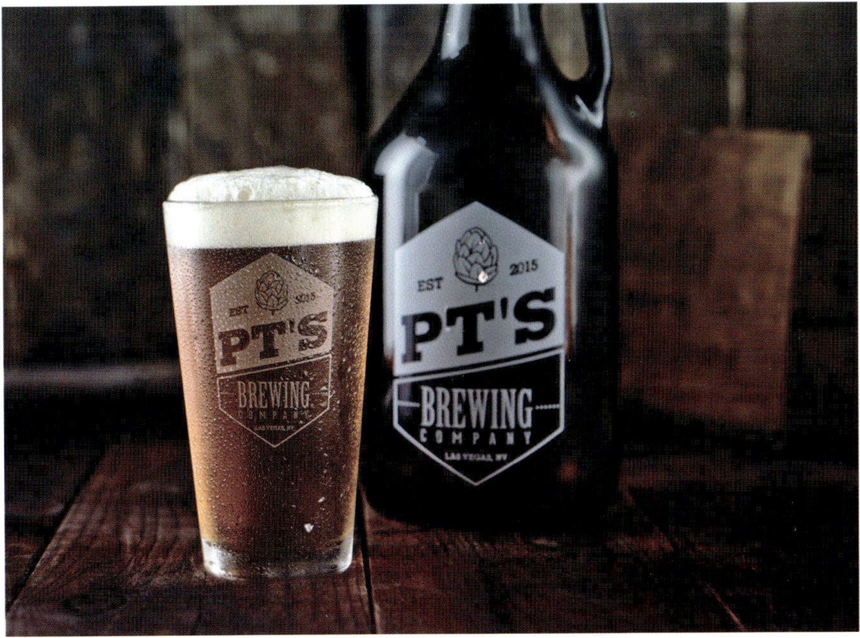

A growler and pint of PT's Brewing Company Hualapai IPA. The brewery won a Great American Beer Festival medal for Boulder Stout. *Courtesy PT's Brewing Company.*

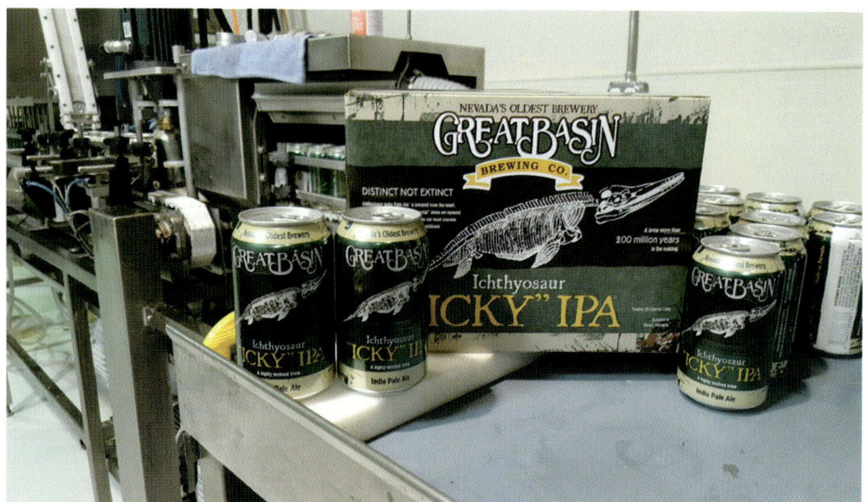

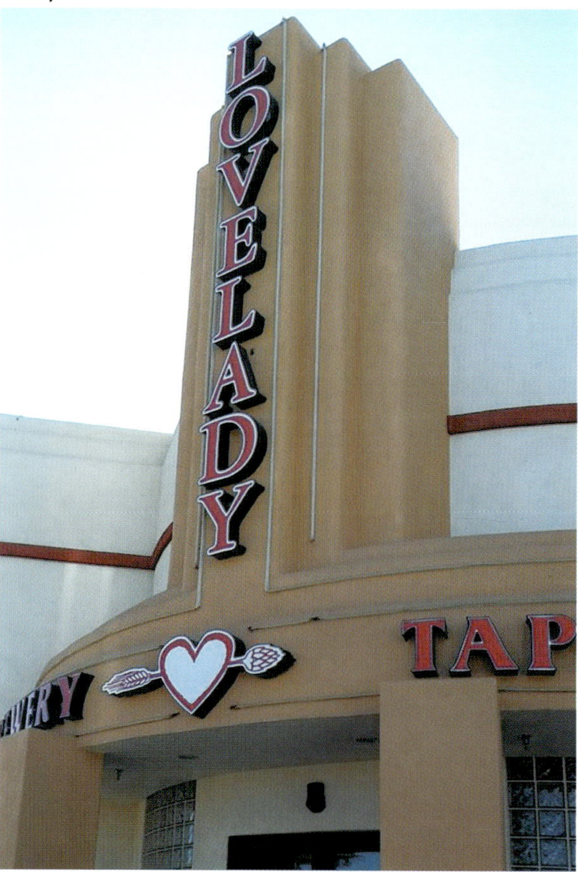

Above: Icthyosaur IPA was considered an extreme beer when it was first brewed as a Great Basin Brewing seasonal. Named after the Nevada state fossil, Icky IPA has become a staple of northern Nevada's beer scene. *Courtesy Great Basin Brewing Company.*

Left: Lovelady Brewing Company opened in 2016. The head brewer, Richard Lovelady, brewed at Gordon Biersch for more than twenty years. *Courtesy Lovelady Brewing Company.*

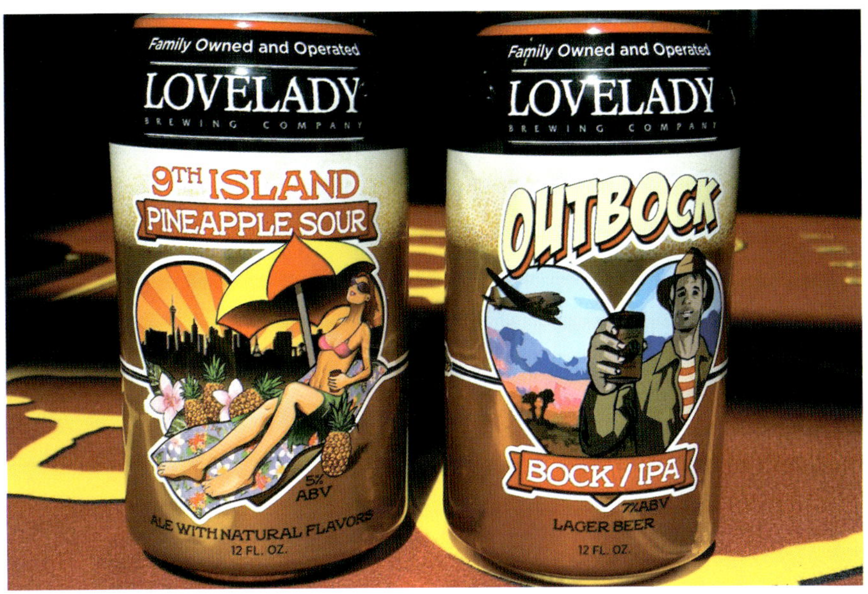

Richard Lovelady set out to brew more inventive beers at his brewery to help set himself apart from his time at Gordon Biersch. *Courtesy Lovelady Brewing Company.*

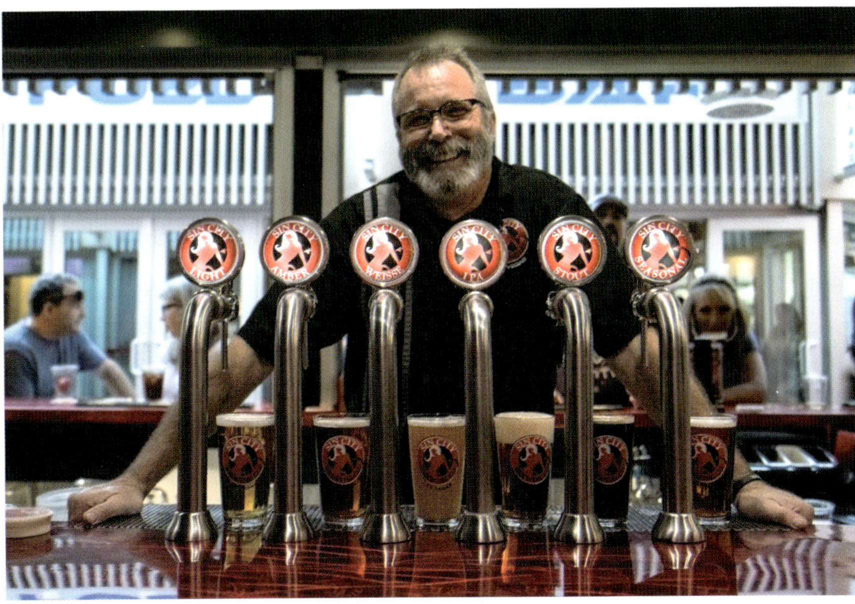

Richard Johnson stands behinds Sin City Brewing tap handles at one of his taprooms. Johnson set out to be the Strip's brewery. *Courtesy Sin City Brewing.*

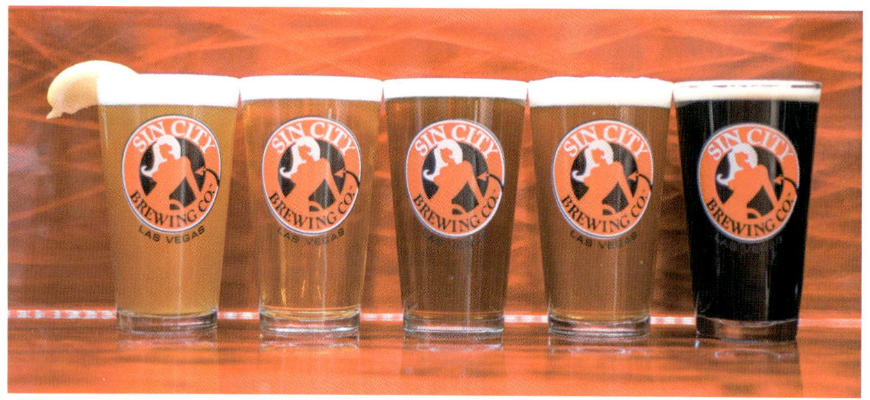

A lineup of Sin City Brewing beers. Johnson, a longtime brewer at Gordon Biersch, brews a classic array of beers, desiring to appeal to the masses who visit the Strip. *Courtesy Sin City Brewing.*

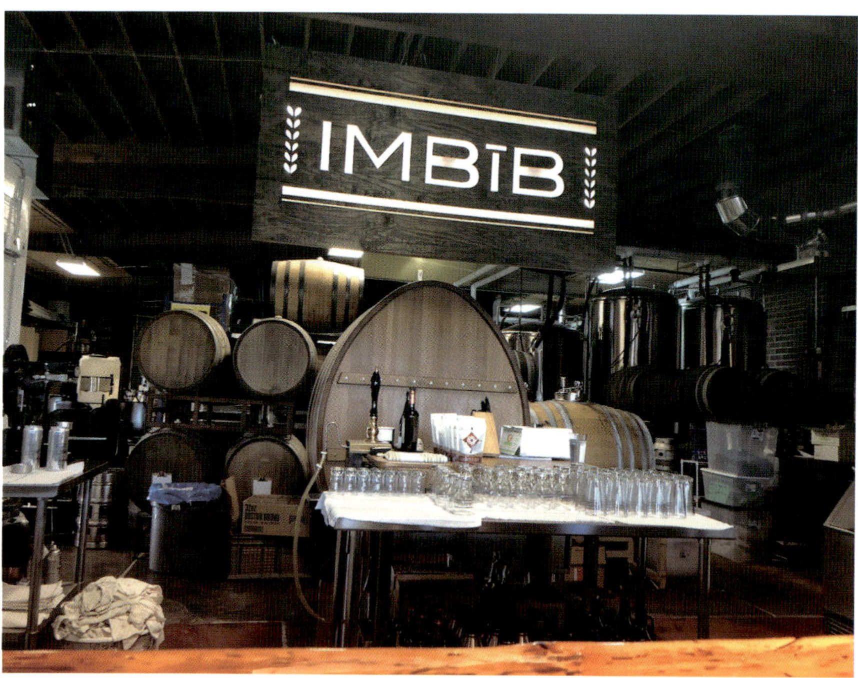

IMBIB Custom Brews opened in 2015 with a 1.5-barrel brewing system. Now operating with a 10-barrel system, the Reno brewery makes a variety of wood-aged and sour beers. *Photo by Pat Evans.*

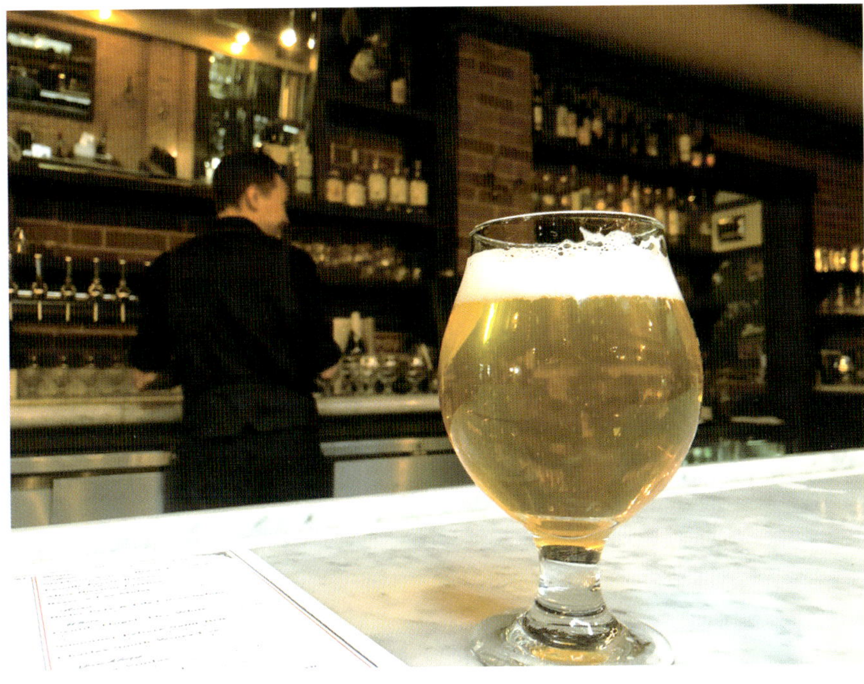

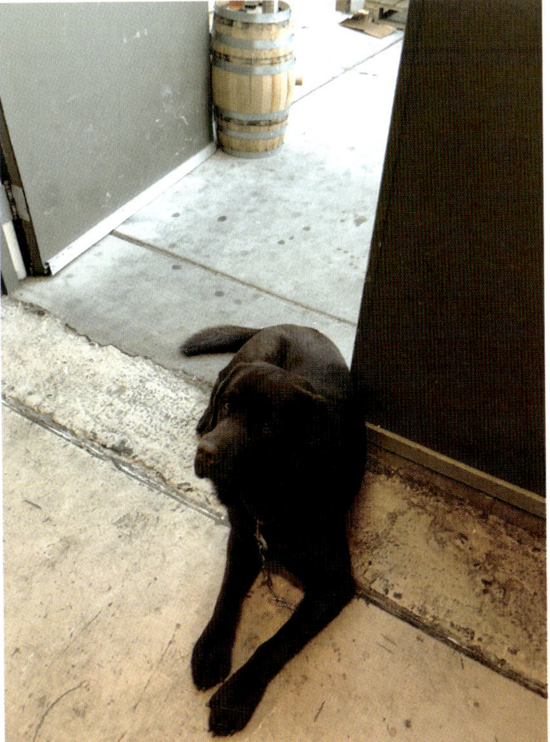

Above: Brasserie Saint James brews a multitude of styles, focusing mainly on French- and Belgian-style beers. In 2014, the Reno brewpub won Mid-Size Brewpub and Mid-Size Brewer of the Year at the Great American Beer Festival. *Photo by Pat Evans.*

Left: The brewery dog at the Depot Craft Brewery Distillery. *Photo by Pat Evans.*

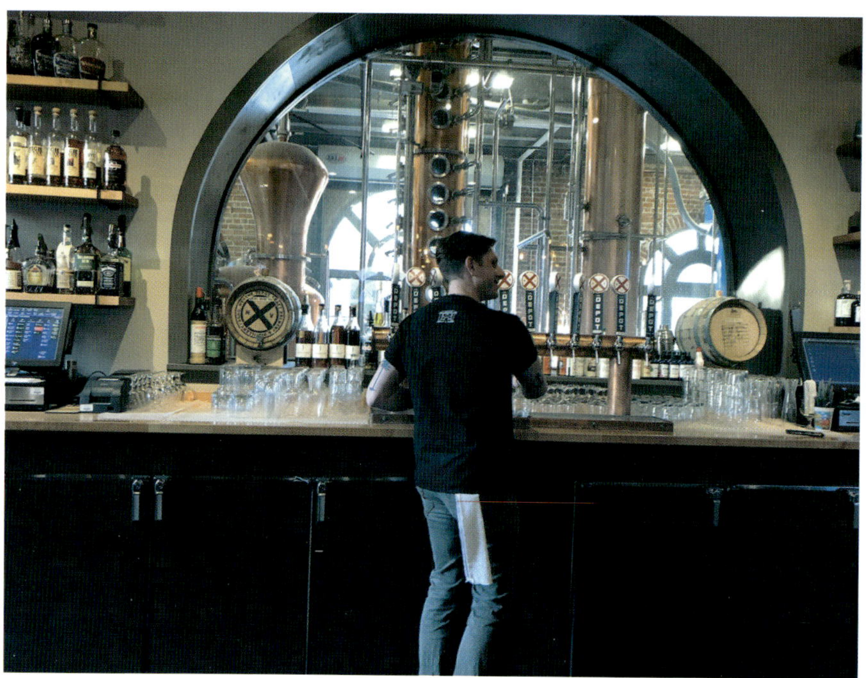

A bartender pours a beer at the Depot Craft Brewery Distillery. Behind the windows, the brewing and distilling takes place. *Photo by Pat Evans.*

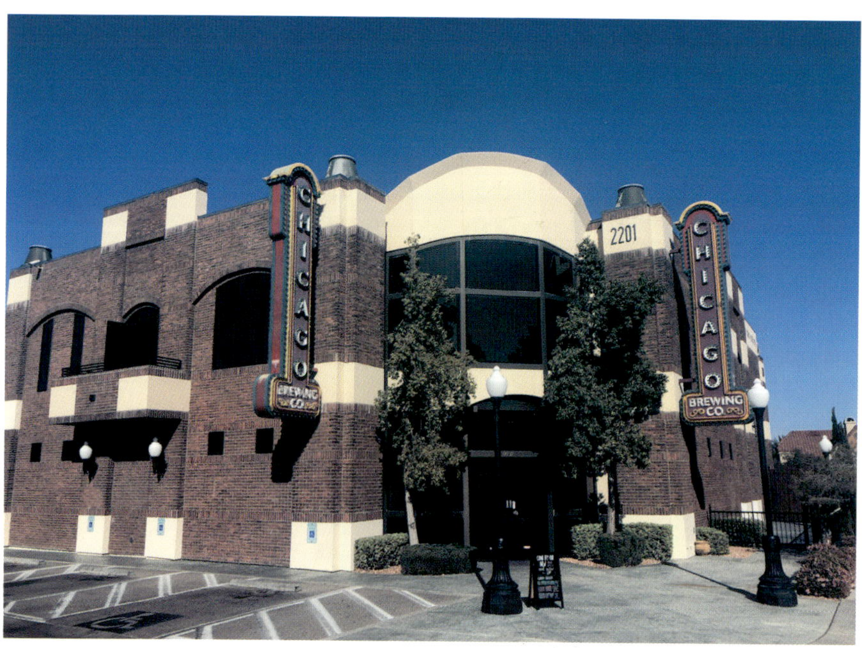

Chicago Brewing Company opened in 1999. The brewery has won more than a dozen major brewing awards. *Photo by Pat Evans.*

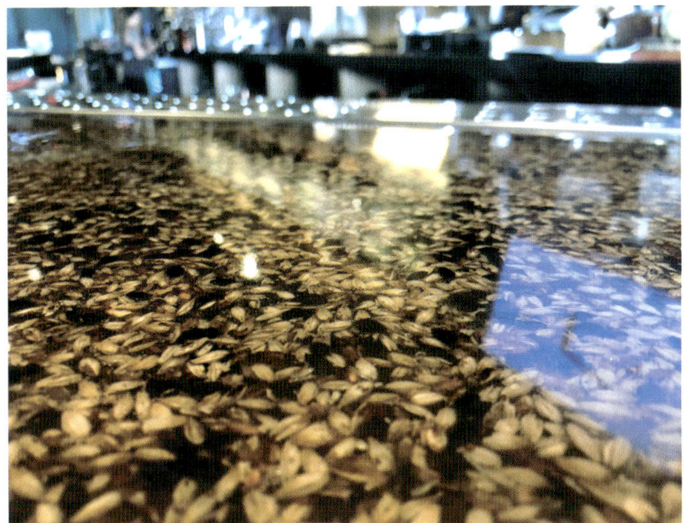

The bar top at Hop Nuts Brewing in downtown Las Vegas. Hop Nuts brews a variety of hop-forward beers but also made waves with its Golden Knights Belgian Strong Ale. *Photo by Pat Evans.*

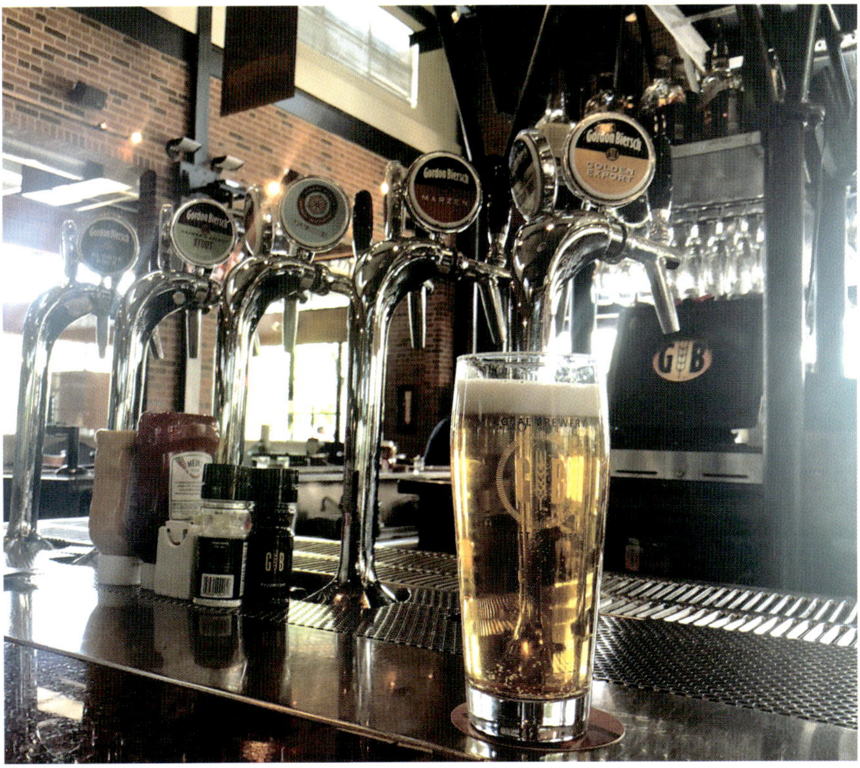

A Gordon Biersch Pilsner on the brewpub's bar in 2018. The brewery won a World Beer Cup in 2014 for its German-style Bock. *Photo by Pat Evans.*

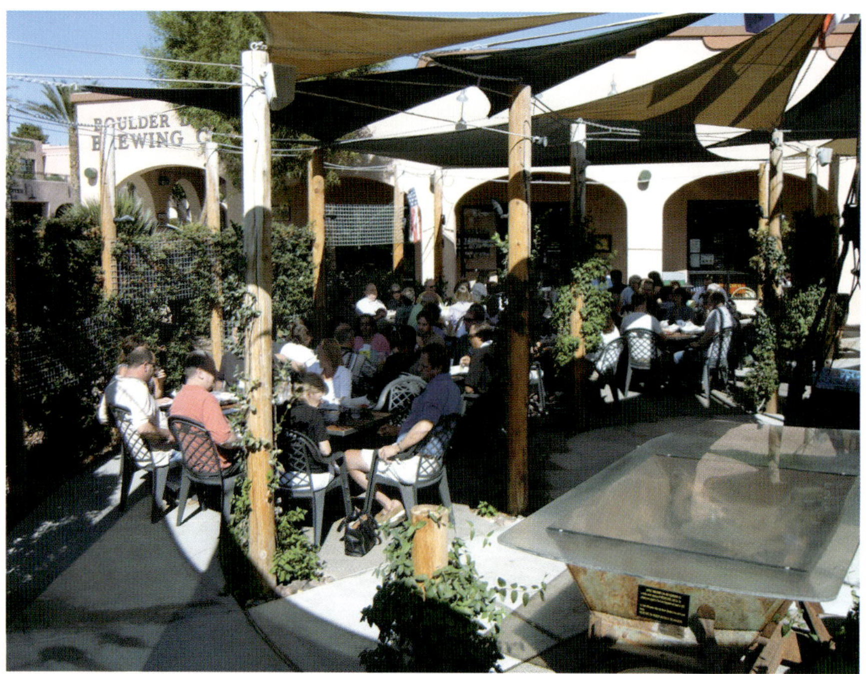

The patio at Boulder Dam Brewing in Boulder City. Todd Cook opened the brewery in 2007 with the small community in mind. *Courtesy of Boulder Dam Brewing.*

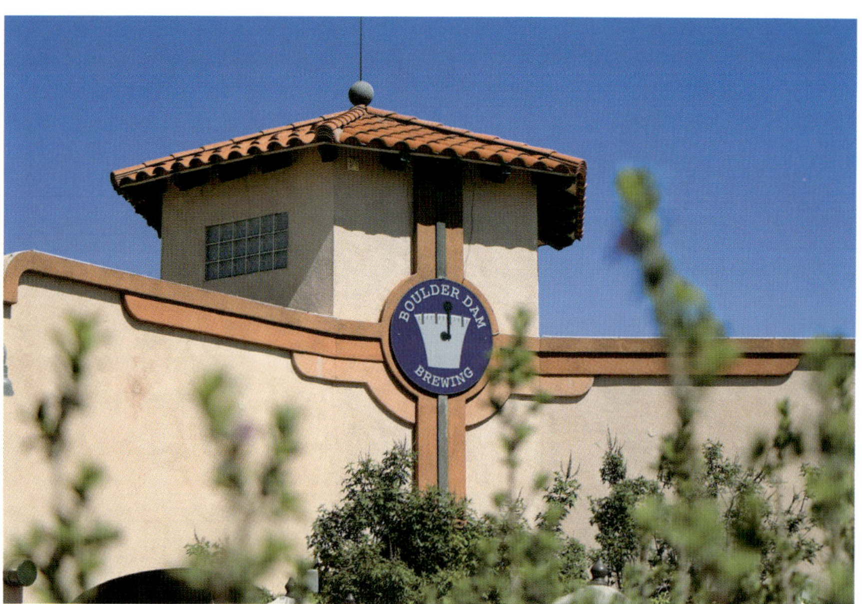

Boulder Dam Brewing's logo overlooks a courtyard in Boulder City. Todd Cook's brewery has been a staple in the southern Nevada community for more than a decade. *Courtesy Boulder Dam Brewing.*

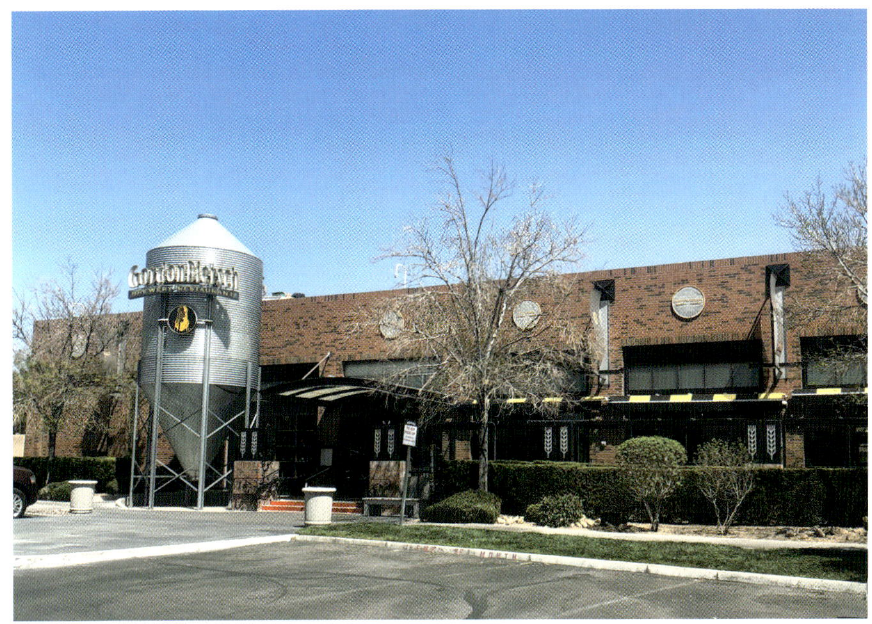

Part of a nationwide chain of brewpubs, Gordon Biersch opened its first free-standing location in 1997, just east of the Strip. Longtime Las Vegas brewers Richard Johnson and Richard Lovelady both brewed at Gordon Biersch. *Photo by Pat Evans.*

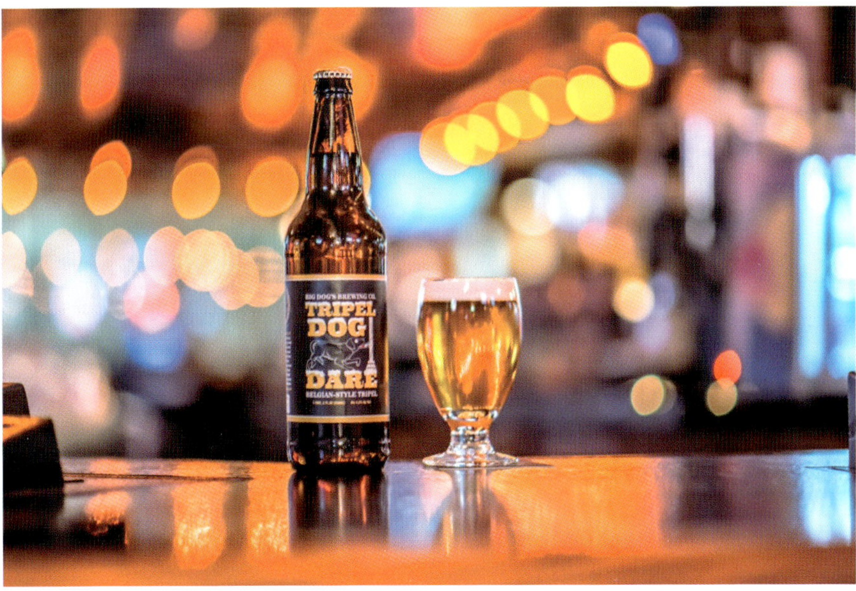

Big Dog's Tripel Dog Dare, a Belgian-style tripel. Tripel Dog Dare won back-to-back Great American Beer Festival medals in 2016 and 2017. *Courtesy Big Dog's Brewing.*

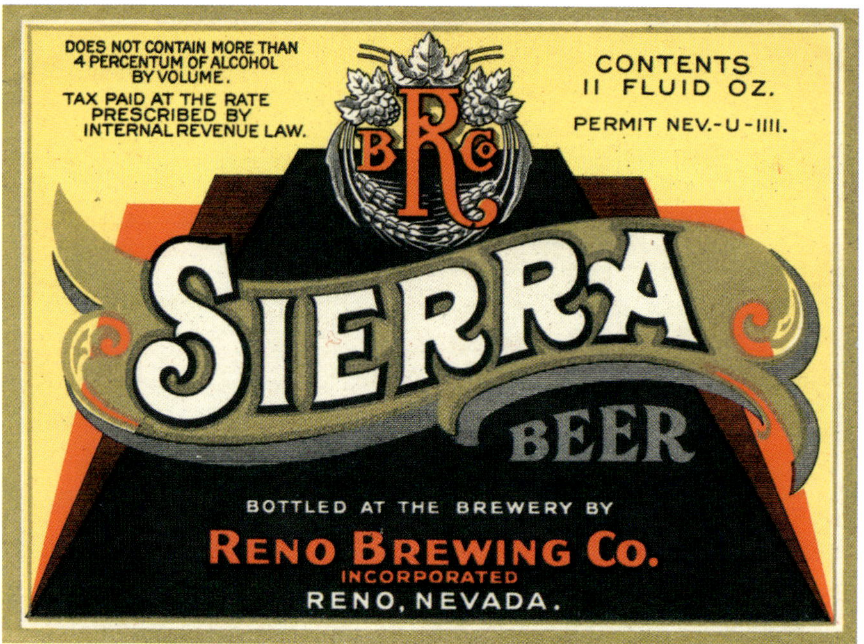

A Sierra Beer label. Sierra Beer was on of the staple brands brewed by Reno Brewing Company. *Author's collection.*

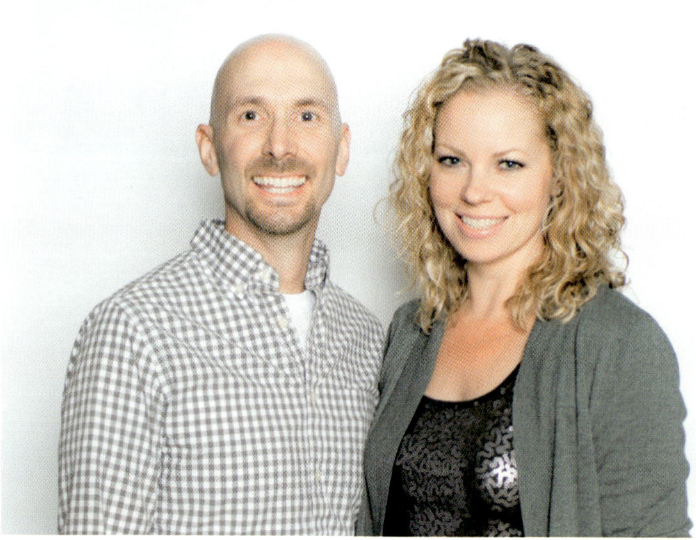

Dave and Wyndee Forrest, the founders of Henderson's Crafthaus Brewery. The Forrests were vital in helping change laws to improve the beer environment in southern Nevada. *Courtesy CraftHaus Brewery.*

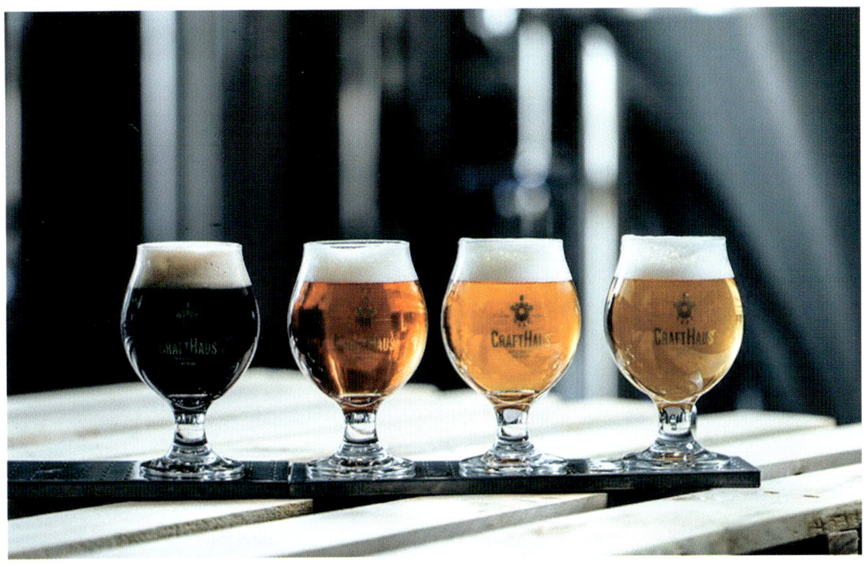

A lineup of Crafthaus Brewery beers. Crafthaus opened with just two flagship beers, looking for quality over quantity. *Courtesy CraftHaus Brewery.*

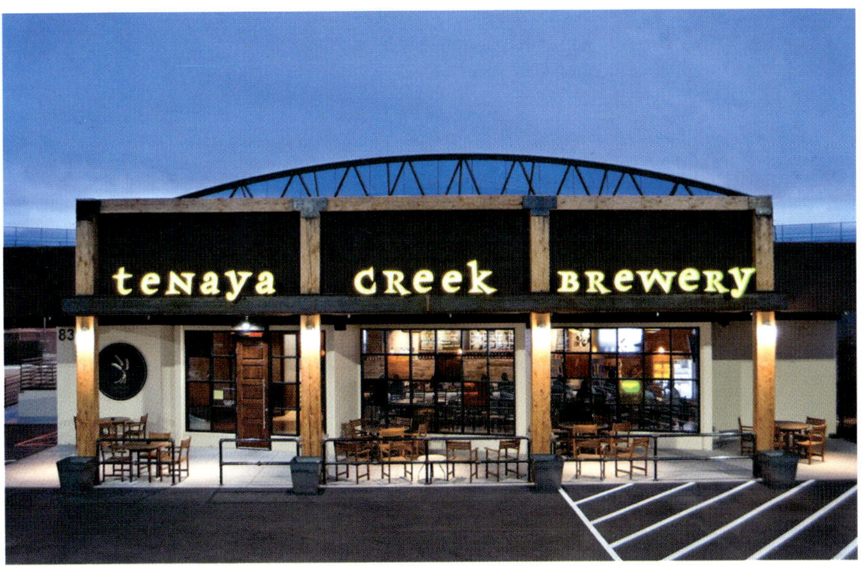

Tenaya Creek Brewery's new location in downtown Las Vegas. The brewery moved when it outgrew its original location. *Courtesy Tenaya Creek Brewery.*

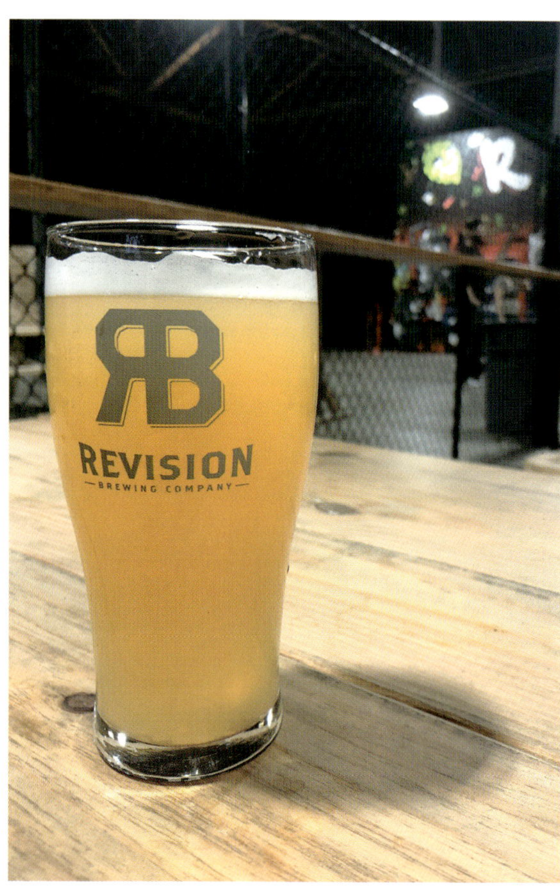

Left: Revision Brewing opened in Sparks with aggressive growth plans. Seasoned IPA brewer Jeremy Warren won two medals at the World Beer Cup in 2018 for Revision IPA and Revision DIPA. *Photo by Pat Evans.*

Below: Big Dog's Brewing Company's exterior. Big Dog's opened in 2002 after moving from its Holy Cow! Casino & Brewery location. *Courtesy Big Dog's Brewing.*

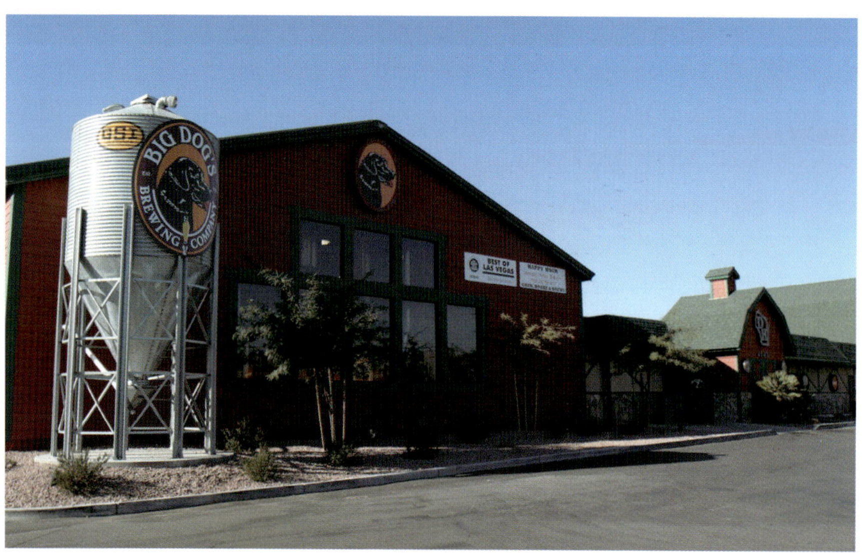

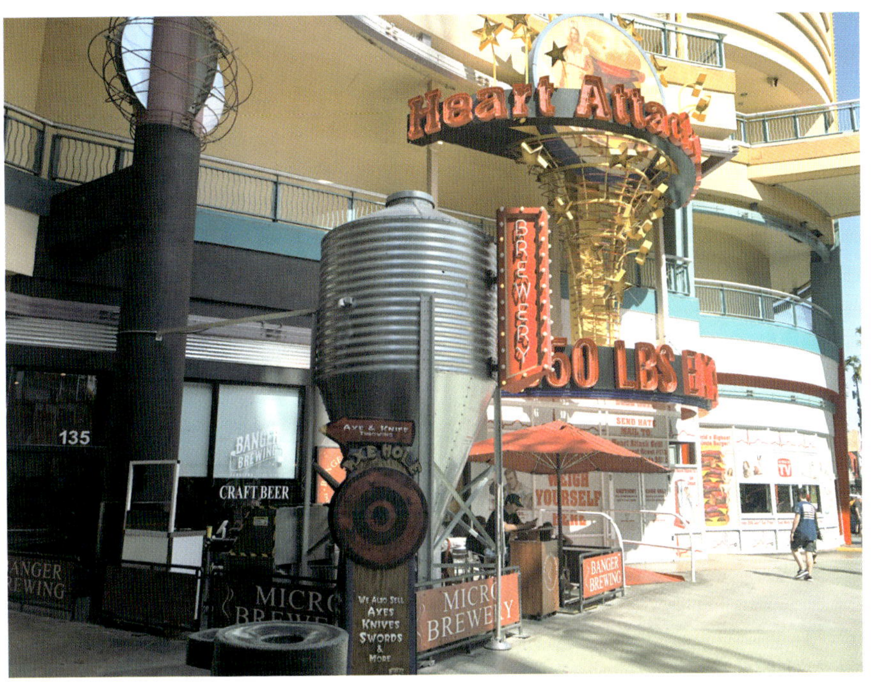

Banger Brewing on Fremont Street in downtown Las Vegas. Banger Brewing's El Heffe is a familiar beer at bars across Las Vegas. *Photo by Pat Evans.*

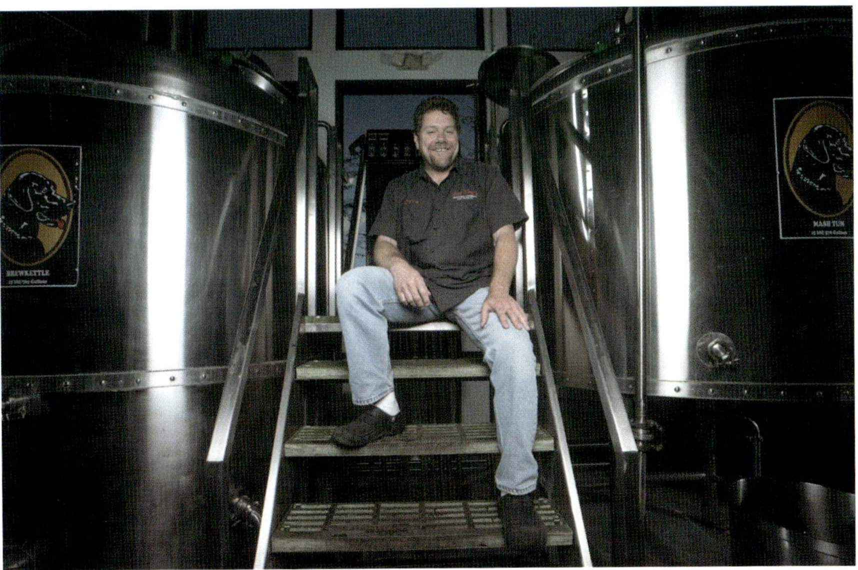

Dave Otto sits on the steps of the brewing system at Big Dog's Brewing. Otto brewed at Big Dog's for nearly twenty years before moving to PT's Brewing Company. *Courtesy Big Dog's Brewing.*

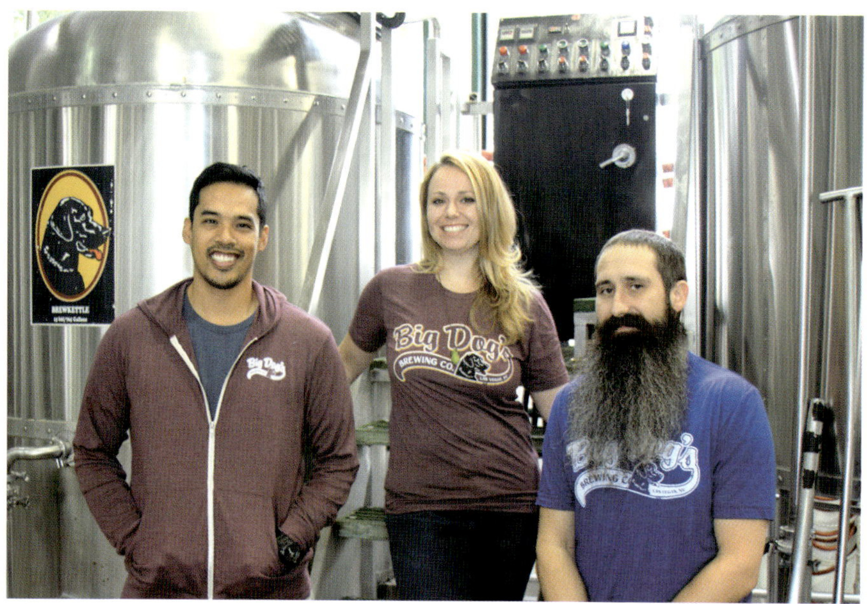

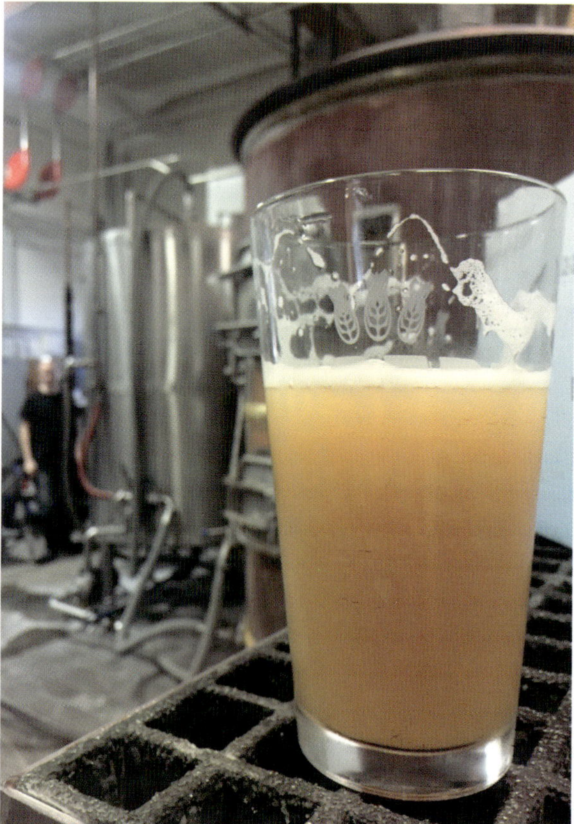

Above: The 2018 Big Dog's Brewing Company brewing team. *From left to right*: David Pascual, Amanda Koeller and Sam McKnney. *Courtesy Big Dog's Brewing.*

Left: A hazy IPA sits on the brewing platform at Joseph James Brewing Company. Brewer Kyle Weinger, *in the background*, came up with the recipe for Citra Rye Pale Ale, a popular Las Vegas beer and GABF medal winner. *Photo by Pat Evans.*

CHAPTER 7

BEER DESERT?

Nevada isn't thought of as a state flush with good beer. For starters, it's a giant piece of land with two population centers and a lot of nothing. Much of America looks at Nevada as a place of immoral depravity. Las Vegas is often seen as a throw-away city with not much to offer aside from debauchery and Reno as a smaller version of the city to the south. Cheap beers are given away on the gambling floors, and restaurants are still largely dominated by cocktail and wine. Beer just doesn't get much mindshare in Nevada.

With craft beer having evolved into a sort of cultural beacon in states across the United States, the beer industry within Nevada has been overlooked and ignored, despite its excellence on national stages. For evidence of such excellence, one doesn't have to look much further than the 2018 World Beer Cup, when two Reno breweries each won two medals. One of those breweries, Revision Brewing, won a gold and silver in two of the hottest categories: IPA and Imperial IPA. The other, Great Basin Brewing, has been a stalwart as Nevada's oldest brewery since Tom Young started brewing in 1993.

The state's beer industry is small, with fewer than forty breweries, but it likely leads the nation in the very unscientific stat of most Great American Beer Festival and World Beer Cup medals per brewery in the United States. Great Basin alone has twenty-two medals at the most prestigious beer competitions. Yet when publications decide to rank states based on their beer scenes, Nevada often finds itself near the bottom.

"We have a world-class beer scene," said David Pascual, the head brewer at Big Dog's Brewing in Las Vegas. "It's all opinion, and sometimes they don't know and clearly it's just from hearsay. It irks me, but it's just more of that fire underneath you. I like the underdog feel; we like to stick it to them."

Most of the brewers in Nevada do make good beer; still, Las Vegas and the state as a whole have lagged behind the top beer states in numbers of breweries and beer trends, said Dave Otto, the head brewer at PT's Brewing Company and former longtime head brewer at Big Dog's.

Otto, who has brewed in Las Vegas since the mid-1990s, can't even put his finger on the reason for the slow development of the beer industry in Nevada. "There's a lot of theories," Otto said. "We really don't have a big beer culture in this town and we never have; [it's] better now than it's ever been, but it still lags behind everywhere I can think of, and I don't know why. Vegas is a real mystery to me."

The most obvious reason for most looking at the state and the reason Otto puts the most stock into is gaming. He said real estate prices in Las Vegas reflect an establishment's ability to have fifteen gaming machines and the expectation that those can make $50,000 a month, almost forcing the hand of a brewpub owner in order to make rent in desirable commercial areas. "For some reason, that just seems to get in the way of cool pubs and taprooms," Otto said. "The breweries that do have their taprooms and no gaming just don't seem to be all that busy all the time. You go to Southern California, and those places are mobbed every day, and I don't understand why that doesn't translate here."

Also tied to gaming, the casino breweries probably hurt Las Vegas early on as, aside from Holy Cow! (now Big Dog's), most of the breweries in the 1990s were within casinos—many of which still survive today. They weren't making the best beer, and even today, most lack innovation and don't push any boundaries, leaving beer fans who seek them out wanting more. Many of the beer menus read like relics from an earlier beer era: lager, pale ale, amber, stout.

"Obviously, we're only as strong as our weakest link, but there's a niche for everyone," Pascual said. "At Big Dog's, we have flexibility to push the envelopes. Those guys have their place, and it's just slowly trying to figure things out. There are some I never thought would brew an IPA, but markets will dictate anything."

It's also been nearly impossible for craft breweries to break into the beer rotation at casino bars and on the gambling floor. Large corporate beverage programs, even without pay-to-play schemes, are hard to appease and want well-known entities to the millions of visitors who hit the Strip each year. Early on, there was little need to bring on craft when the beer market share was well under 5 percent. Even as the market share grew, casinos wanted people to drink more weaker beers, said Clyde Burney, vice president of beer and trade development at Southern Glazer's Wine & Spirits.

"The early days, I was told numerous times, 'Clyde, I know you have great selection, but we're not interested,'" Burney said. "It's a little different now, because there's schmucks like me who have upset it a little bit."

In 2018, the Strip is much more welcoming of craft beers. There are restaurants like Tom's Urban, Robert Irvine's Public House and Yardbird that all offer a wide selection of beers, many of which are brewed locally. It was announced as this book was sent to publisher a brewpub would open at the Palazzo, connected to California's Trustworthy Brewing Co.

It was through efforts like those of Burney, who has brought many of the major craft brands into Nevada, such as Sierra Nevada and Firestone Walker, that they have been able to make waves.

Burney is also quick to point to the strength of the growing scene in Reno, with proximity to Northern California's beer scene and award-winning breweries like Great Basin and Brasserie Saint James, along with upstarts like Revision.

Then there's Sarah Johnson, now a Ninkasi Brewing executive in Oregon but a longtime beverage executive at Mandalay Bay Resort and Casino. She saw an opportunity on the Strip in 2011, knowing the growing trend of beer and acknowledging the lack of offerings on Las Vegas Boulevard. She said brewers understanding of the beer culture in Las Vegas weren't there and weren't super interested, so she spent time building relationships and convincing them that customers in Las Vegas were demanding flavorful beers.

Still, it wasn't easy, especially internally. "It was a lot of people to convince and a lot of people to turn a ship, and I was getting frustrated," she said. "I really wanted to make a move, and I picked Lagunitas IPA and put it on the floor as a free comp beer. It was probably a mistake."

She acknowledges it probably wasn't the right craft beer to start with for free beers on the floor and that customers would want more flavorful beers but had learned not to expect them at casinos.

Eventually, it gained traction, and she built an extremely successful corporate beverage program with beer and even held massive beer festivals to celebrate it.

"Craft will continue to keep growing here," Burney said. "Bring it to your lips, smell it, taste it. That's why I think local will continue to keep growing."

Beyond the casino breweries, legal challenges posed a major problem for potential startups. Gaming adds a high cost to potential taprooms and a factor unusual to beer lovers from states outside Nevada—gaming computers at the bar—but taprooms in Las Vegas like Hop Nuts Brewing and Tenaya Creek have moved past that stigma.

Head south a few minutes to Henderson, an independent city, and the breweries are more along the lines of the taprooms the rest of the country is familiar with, thanks to the efforts of Wyndee and Dave Forrest of CraftHaus Brewery in 2013. The couple was instrumental in changing the city's brewpub licensing so they didn't have to pay the $60,000 fee to operate a taproom, which included the gaming license.

Since the change, multiple breweries have opened in Henderson, including Bad Beat Brewing and Lovelady Brewing. Joseph James Brewing, a production-only brewery, is also located in Henderson.

Before the modern craft beer explosion, Las Vegas was similar to other cities but fell behind, said Richard Lovelady, who owns Lovelady Brewing with his brothers and brewed for more than two decades at Gordon Biersch Brewing Company in Las Vegas.

"For a long time, nothing changed. Even into the early 2000s, it seemed like we had more breweries than San Diego," said Lovelady, who was a regional manager with Gordon Biersch. "Then, five years later, we had the same and San Diego took off. I'd travel to a different market every six months, and they'd all have two to three new breweries, and I'd come back and nothing changed here, every time. Now we're starting to see the signs. We're still way behind everywhere else on the West Coast and most of the country, but I can start to see it coming."

A lack of a clear-cut downtown and growing sprawl could hamper the outside view, but the growth Las Vegas has experienced in the past twenty to thirty years will likely lead to a changed perception. The city is no longer just a city of sins. It now has a diversifying economy; an evolving, homegrown culinary scene outside the Strip; and a thriving sports community rallied by the record-shattering first-year NHL franchise Vegas Golden Knights and soon to be joined by the Oakland Raiders when they move to town in 2020.

It took the city longer than most to mature and move beyond its gaming and party image, a reputation it still struggles with, for better or worse. The beer scene has followed, with a solid base and bright future.

"We do have a small community, but also we're all working that uphill battle," Pascual said. "We all can relate really well. As a brewer, I felt at one point like I was on an island. Then, talking to them and getting to know them, they all got what I'm going through. We're all in the same boat, fighting for the same thing to make our brands and beer successful."

CHAPTER 8

DIRTY GAMES

In the 1980s and 1990s, as Las Vegas geared up and doubled down on its tourism efforts, casinos and resorts pulled every string they could to get people to come to town. It was in this era when the idea of free rooms, free drinks, upgrades and the cost of amenities was thrown out the window. It was also in this era that Budweiser and Miller became the dominant players in town, as prior, Coors Brewing was the prominent mass beer producer in Nevada.

As happens when businesses give enough value away, they began to feel it in the books, so they began to tighten their purse strings and look for ways to generate revenue. This was the beginning of pay-to-play for beverage—and presumably other—suppliers, and the first such beverage program was implemented at Harrah Entertainment, according to an anonymous former Anheuser-Busch salesman who dealt extensively with casinos. The casino group would charge the brewer two dollars per case sold, and in turn, the brewer would earn preferred, and in some cases exclusive, rights to distribution within the gaming company's properties.

Initially, Anheuser-Busch scoffed at the request and declined to pay the fees. The gaming company was not bluffing, and Budweiser was gone from the taps and shelves at Harrah establishments for two years until Budweiser complied.

According to the salesman, as long as the fees were paid by the brewer—in this case Anheuser-Busch—the tactic was legal. Eventually, all of the casino groups fell into line, and the fees for a brewer like Anheuser-Busch could climb to more than $4 million a year.

Anheuser-Busch paid into the programs to ensure it wouldn't lose market share to its main competition, Miller Brewing. This revenue-generating tactic and its limited legal restrictions and enforcement have had reverberating effects on the craft industry in Nevada.

The pay-to-play fees don't stop at the casinos; they run deep into the off-premise retailers as well, according to the former salesman. These fees, along with the general dominance of casinos as the entertainment venues in Las Vegas, lead to plenty of anecdotal experiences from small brewers in the state. While few are provable, and more are completely legal through loopholes, there is a tangible distrust of big brewers and the big entertainment companies by the small brewers in the state.

The state's beer and liquor distributors are not allowed to participate in the pay-to-play schemes; however, they do, according to the salesman. The distributors do so by shuffling money to the supplier, as well as hiding payments by way of sponsorships to establishments. Any laws on the books about pay-to-play are also not well enforced in Las Vegas and Nevada, according to a liquor law attorney in the state.

That's not to say there haven't been well-documented cases regarding the practice. Most notable was a crackdown by the Alcohol and Tobacco Tax and Trade Bureau in 2011, when the department accepted a compromise of $1.9 million from six companies accused of violating the slotting fee provision of the Federal Alcohol Administration Act.

Diageo North America, Pernod Ricard USA, Moet Hennessey, Bacardi, Future Brands and E.&J. Gallo Winery were all part of the settlement agreements and, with the payments, denied violating any rules. The accusations stemmed from the companies' involvement in Harrah Entertainment's Nationwide Beverage Program, which solicited better placements in its bars in exchange for payment and received nearly $2 million through a third party.

A beer executive at a Las Vegas distributor said the crackdowns do happen occasionally, but in general, beer-slotting fees are perceived as legal as long as the breweries pay them. The distributor agreed with the former Budweiser salesman, saying pay-to-play evolved because of a need and desire for revenue from casinos and competition among the brewery conglomerates intensified the practice.

In 2014, Nevada's attorney general released a memo reminding wholesalers, retailers and suppliers that

> *Nevada, like most states, prohibits certain transactions and relationships between retailers, wholesalers and suppliers.*
>
> *Perhaps the most significant restrictions apply to wholesalers and retailers. Among other things, a wholesaler may not "loan any money or other thing of value to," "invest money, directly or indirectly in," "furnish or provide any premises, building, bar or equipment to" or "participate, directly or indirectly, in the operation of the business of a retailer."*

The memo also noted that suppliers could not require wholesalers split profits, accept delivery that wasn't ordered or set prices after delivery.

Perhaps most confusing and frustrating for the small brewers are situations like the Beer Park by Budweiser at Paris Las Vegas. Essentially a tied house, which are illegal, Beer Park is a bar on the Strip with a beer menu dominated by AB InBev products. There are several independent craft breweries represented on the menu, mostly distributed by the city's Budweiser distributor. The bar is effectively sponsored by AB InBev, the Belgian company that now owns Anheuser-Busch, but the supplier does not share any profits from the establishment. Basically, Beer Park is a giant billboard for the brewery right on the Strip, across from the famed Bellagio fountains, according to the former salesman who is no longer with the company.

There is a law on the books forbidding exclusive relationships with one distributor. In Las Vegas, AB InBev is assisted by franchise laws that kept its brands in separate distributors, so beers like Stella Artois and Budweiser are sold by different companies.

Distributors in Las Vegas talk openly, albeit largely anonymously, about the pay-to-play practices. Along with knowing that the larger companies can pay, casinos don't want strong beers in their casinos, said Clyde Burney, vice president of beer and trade development at Southern Glazer's Wine & Spirits. Southern Glazer's largest beer brands are Corona and Modelo, but Burney said he still feels the pressure when he tries to get his brands into different establishments.

"They want you drinking more beers at a better price," Burney said of the casinos. "You can tell by the properties. The guys swimming against the tide, that's who we target."

Burney acknowledged that the larger craft brewers have grown to a size where they, too, can compete in the pay-to-play schemes but said that overall the practice is mostly between the two big companies. It hurts the small breweries, especially locally. One Nevada craft brewery executive said he has run into pay-to-play tactics from a national craft brewer. Those practices remain limiting to the state's craft brewers, especially so long as casinos offer up the in-demand free drinks.

"You have casinos giving away macro beers still," said David Pascual, the director of brewing operations at Big Dog's Brewing. "They're not doing that with a $200 keg we might sell, but they'll do it with an $80."

CHAPTER 9

BRINGING BREWERIES BACK

Once Carson Brewing Company and Reno Brewing Company closed in the middle of the twentieth century, Nevada was completely void of beer making. It wasn't until 1987 that brewing was brought back to Nevada, and fittingly in Virginia City. Rick and Julie Hoover were successfully able to lobby the state to allow for a brewery in historic districts where brewing once took place. The law was limiting, as only five hundred barrels a year could be brewed. With the new law, the Hoovers were able to open the Union Brewery Saloon where Charles Baker once brewed beer. According to a 1991 *Reno Gazette-Journal* article, the building was a brewery until 1897, but most records indicate the property served mostly as a saloon until Rick Hoover purchased the building in 1985 and eventually was bet by a customer that he couldn't legally brew beer.

At the time, only eighteen states allowed for brewpubs, and according to the *Gazette-Journal*, Hoover's permission only came via "a narrow exception," with the disclaimer that it would be of "cultural, educational, historic and general welfare of the public."

Once the new law was passed, Hoover began brewing forty-five gallons of beer a week in the basement of the building. Often, he was out within a few days, he told the *Gazette-Journal*. "People are just tired of the regular beers you can buy in the liquor store," he said in 1991 in an article about the passing of a wider brewpub bill. "They want something with taste and body."

With the passing of the historic brewpub law, there was a national undercurrent to change laws, in part led by Bill Owens from California, who owned Buffalo Bill's brewpub and started a political action committee. "The wave is coming," Owens said in 1987. "I think we'll see a major revolution in brewing in the next five years."

Owens was probably more right than he knew, as 1988 ushered in a class of breweries across the United States that would be among the most influential of the modern age of beer. From 1965—when Fritz Maytag purchased San Francisco's Anchor Brewing—to 1988, fewer than eighty breweries opened. In 1988, more than fifty-five opened, including Goose Island, Rogue, Deschutes, North Coast, Great Lakes Brewing and Brooklyn Brewing.

It wasn't long before Hoover's quantities and tight brewing space no longer made sense, but before he was finished, several upstarts were well underway.

A fire closed Hoover's business in 1996, and he sold Union Brewery to Tom Graham, who planned to begin brewing again in 1997.

Homebrewing

As with most of the rest of the nation, the spur in the brewing industry and eventual shift from macro light lagers like Budweiser and Miller, was a surge in homebrewing. Thanks to a law passed by President Jimmy Carter in October 1978, homebrewing became legal, and with seemingly thousands of people realizing better beer was made overseas, a massive cultural movement had its roots. Add in the visionary and advocate that was Charlie Papazian, and the trend was underway. Papazian founded the American Homebrewers Association and the Association of Brewers, as well as the Great American Beer Festival. In 1984, Papazian released *Complete Joy of Home Brewing*, which is still in print and has sold nearly one million copies as the "home brewer's bible."

By 1986, the homebrew bug was a business opportunity in Nevada. A 1986 *Reno Gazette-Journal* story highlighted the growing import market, pegged on the recent entrance and 200 percent surge of Corona Extra in the United States, but packaged a story about the Reno homebrewing market as well. At the time, there were two homebrew stores that had recently opened in Reno: Beer Essentials by Andrew "Tony" Smith and Reno Homebrewer by Rob Bates.

"Smith says he advocates home brewing because the product is better than mass produced beer and it's less expensive," the *Gazette-Journal* summarized.

Bates opened Reno Homebrewer in the summer of 1986 with his wife, Elaine, with the idea that homebrewing opportunities were limitless because of the "thin, fizzy mouthwash" that dominated the beer market in the 1980s. The couple left jobs in Silicon Valley to open the homebrew store. Reno Homebrewer sold a forty-five-dollar starter kit. Beer Essentials' version was fifty dollars.

The same article mentioned the Washoe Zephyr Zymurgists, the region's homebrewing club.

Homebrewing was the subject of a large story featuring Bates in 1993, all about how to get started. The story also featured the publisher of *Nevada Magazine*, Rich Moreno, a novice brewer, and KOLO Channel 8 anchorman Ed Pearce, a brewer of five years who made Cousin Jack beer with his brother.

"It was kind of a fun project when I first started but I was surprised at how good a beer you can make," Pearce told the *Gazette-Journal*. "You can just about make a better beer than you can buy and if you like beer and it's more than something you just guzzle by the six-pack while watching football with friends, then it's interesting."

Bates was still at it twenty-two years later when the *Gazette-Journal* featured Reno Homebrewer in 2018, following a relocation to Fourth Street, a haven for the modern brewing startups. His daughter Karen Bates had joined him as owner and manager of the store.

"We ran out of space on Dickerson Road. We were trying to run a retail business out of an old warehouse," Bates said. "We couldn't show everything we had available. Now, everything we carry is on the shelf."

The new space allowed Reno Homebrewer to showcase dozens of varieties of hops and malts—both ingredients seeing a massive increase in diversity since the early days of Bates's business—as well as strains of yeasts and brewing equipment.

Carson City and Reno

As Hoover was up and running essentially through a loophole, Dick Murray was ready to open a brewpub in Carson City and Tom Young was prepping sites in the Reno-Sparks area.

The first brewpub in Carson City wasn't Murray's but the Carson Depot, by Al Gasper, in 1993. Gasper served four beers: Griz Ale, Wabuska Wheat Ale, Roundhouse Red Ale and Kati Dark Porter.

By 1994, the *Gazette-Journal* reported the Carson Depot was frequented by plenty of customers. In 1999, the Carson Depot became a "Sports Bar–Chinese Food–Brewery," and in a 1999 *Gazette-Journal* story, an Asian-style lager and a pale ale were expected. The restaurant review applauded the Chinese food.

Despite the apparently tasty Chinese cuisine, Carson Depot was closed by 2001. Another brewery with little on record that came and went in the late 1990s was Carson Valley Brewery.

TASTINGS

In December 1995, a beer tasting was held by *Gazette-Journal* reporter Sandra Macias with certified beer judges Ron Badley and local homebrew shop owner Rob Bates conducting tastings of the three Reno–Carson City area breweries.

Brew Brothers, at the Eldorado Hotel and Casino, scored in the mid-forties—or excellent, according to the American Homebrew Association's scale—for Double Down Stout and Redhead Amber Ale.

"This is a really great stout," Badley said of the stout. "It's difficult to make a stout with the complexity and flavor that this one has."

Great Basin Brewing also scored in the forties for Wild Horse Ale and Jackpot Porter.

The judges also reviewed the Trail's End Smoked Porter by Great Basin Brewing, which used smoked mahogany and apple woods from brewer Eric McClary's home. "It's a labor-intensive beer," Bates said, also writing "rich and satisfying" on his judging sheet.

Carson Depot scored the worst, in the low thirties, which signified as very good, but at the lowest end they judged, for Kati Porter and Griz Ale. While Carson Depot's beers were said to have gotten four thumbs up by the judges, it scored among the worst. "It's more full-bodied than Miller Light," Bates said.

All in all, however, the Reno area was found to have quality beers for the mid-1990s.

"We should count ourselves lucky for the quality of local fresh-made brews," Badley said.

PART IV

MODERN PIONEERS

CHAPTER 10

GREAT BASIN BREWING COMPANY

We argue with Tom about who was first. We had brewpub license no. 3, and they had brewpub license no. 2, but we opened before they did.
—Robert Snyder, Big Dog's Brewing CFO

The U.S. craft beer industry is full of genuine people, but few are as friendly, open and passionate about beer as Tom Young. Like so many of the brewers who have started the more than six thousand breweries in 2018, Young didn't set out in his career to make beer. He had been interested in brewing since childhood, but a career in mining sidetracked him for a few decades.

His memories stretch back to his father sitting in an ugly yellow living room chair, kicking back and teaching him how to pour beer into a glass. "He kept telling me how to pour beer into a proper glass, which was this cross between a pilsner- and goblet-type glass," Young said. "I'd sip it and try to note the flavors, but all the beers were pretty much a fizzy yellow beer."

Being in northern Ohio, his father's go-to beer was Stroh's, and Tom would make note of the label: "Fire brewed for flavor." Throughout those early years, Young would sample beers, though they were all mostly the same, but he'd note the marketing language from each packaging. Following high school, Young earned a scholarship for diving to Florida State, but some trouble with a coaching coup made him finish his degree in Arizona. On a road trip back to Ohio following graduation, Young and friends stopped and bought a beer brand from each state for a party back home.

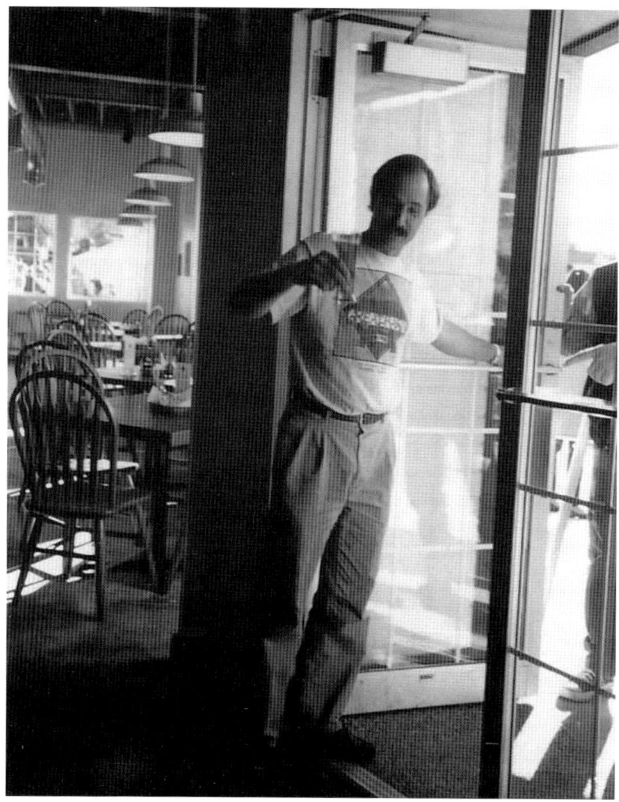

Great Basin Brewing Company founder Tom Young welcomes patrons to the newly opened brewery in Sparks. *Courtesy Great Basin Brewing.*

The true takeaway of his college experience—aside from a master's degree in geological engineering—was the beginnings of his home booze-making. First, they made wine, which according to Young was horrible. Still, since he loved beer, he began experimenting with homebrewing.

"It was here and there, but the ingredients were hard to come across," he said. "Hops were just sold as hops. I didn't know there were varieties. But beer got better as I got more serious."

Young's a-ha moment came, however, in Yugoslavia as a working geologist. He'd see the workers in the mines, a somber bunch of low-paid, hardworking people. At night, there was a transformation. "They seemed so miserable all day, but at night, they'd go to their restaurants and pubs and eat sausages and drink some really fun, delightful beers," he said. "This turned this dismal society into real people."

With the Yugoslavian experience under his belt, he began buying expensive imported beers. Eventually, the costs made his wife find a two-dollar six-pack she brought home, insisting that beer was good enough. Instead of settling for the cheaper beer, Young began taking homebrewing seriously again, taking copious amounts of notes and using his science degrees to better his process and products. He'd use the economic savings as a way to convince his wife to keep it going. As he got better at brewing, more friends would come over and drink, and he'd have to make more and more beer. Eventually, the costs no longer were a benefit, but he kept it going, brewing traditional styles, reproducing them to the best of his ability and experimenting with them. He'd either brew a small one-gallon batch with interesting ingredients or he'd brew a five-gallon base batch, splitting it into five one-gallon fermenters and trying them out with different herbs and fruits.

For a long time, he only could get ingredients through a homebrew catalogue, until a homebrewing store opened in Reno, where he was living at the time. "All of a sudden, there was a gathering space for people like me," he said. "We started a state fair competition, and we didn't know what we were doing. There was a judging panel for porters, and one of the judges gave them a really low score because she didn't like porters. It's like, well that's not the point of beer judging. But I started winning more and more competitions, subscribing to every journal I could and visiting microbreweries as they opened whenever I could."

He wasn't always in the best place to try breweries. As he likes to say, they don't always put a mine next to a nice city. With a lot of time on his hands, sitting in the nicest hotel in Battle Mountain or Pioche, Nevada, away from his family and thinking he shouldn't be traveling so much, he'd start writing a business plan. Eventually, he was on the California side of the California-Nevada border helping set up a new gold mine, and the parent company fell on hard times and decided to sell off its mining assets. "I was the last employee of the company," he said. "I got three months' severance pay and [was] stuck in a tiny town in California with a house we couldn't sell."

He pondered the thought of launching a brewery but knew it was illegal at the time in Nevada, so he thought maybe he'd stay in California. Mining was changing, and the American mining industry was beginning to flounder. His colleagues began shifting overseas to Asia and South America.

"I had a good reputation and I probably could have done that, but my kids were five and seven at the time, and I'm just not sure I wanted to move to Bolivia," he said. "Maybe it would have been fun. But breweries! I was still an avid homebrewer and had won some major blue ribbons, including top honors at the American Homebrewers Association national competition. There's a lot of luck in competition, but if you make a good beer, you could get lucky," Young said. "But I felt like hot stuff."

Great Basin's Start

Once he had decided a brewery was in his future, Young started working with a few other aspirational brewery owners to help get the law changed in Nevada to allow for brewpubs. Eventually, the state passed such a law but made challenging rules, such as breweries had to be in redevelopment districts and faced strict barrelage limits.

"We got it passed, so now I was finally thinking, 'OK, maybe we should do this,'" Young said. "Unfortunately, I don't have a rich uncle and I married for love, so I couldn't just snap my fingers and do it."

With mock business plans in the past, Young decided to shift from a production brewery model to a taproom-based plan, as the Napa Valley model of wineries seemed to prove it could work. As he and a colleague from the mining industry, a self-described wine snob, searched for a location, they found another beer entrepreneur from the mining industry who had investors and a leased location. But an issue arose: the investors weren't beer people, and neither was the head of the company; they just thought the business idea would do well, as it was in neighboring states. They hadn't done the math right in the leased space, and Young, partnering with them, was able to get out of the lease.

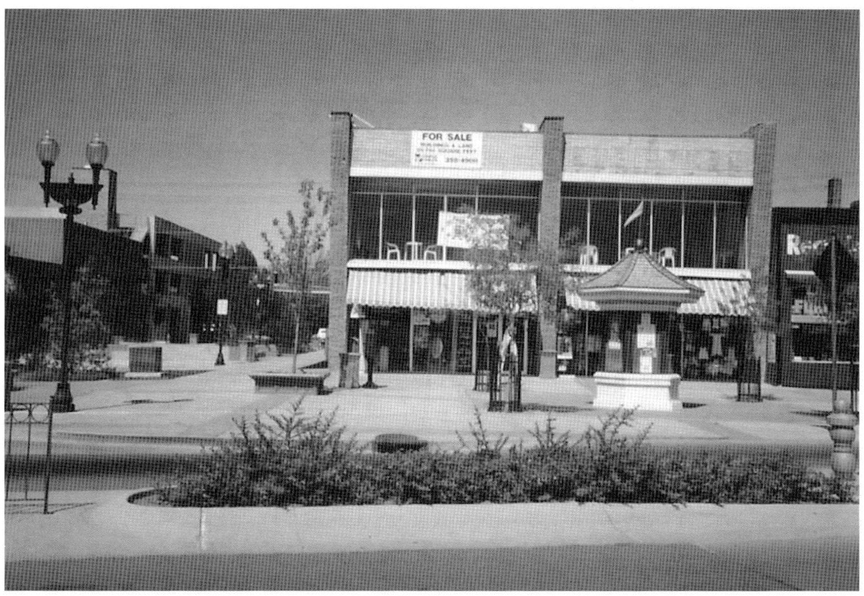

The commercial building in Sparks that Great Basin found for its brewery. *Courtesy Great Basin Brewing.*

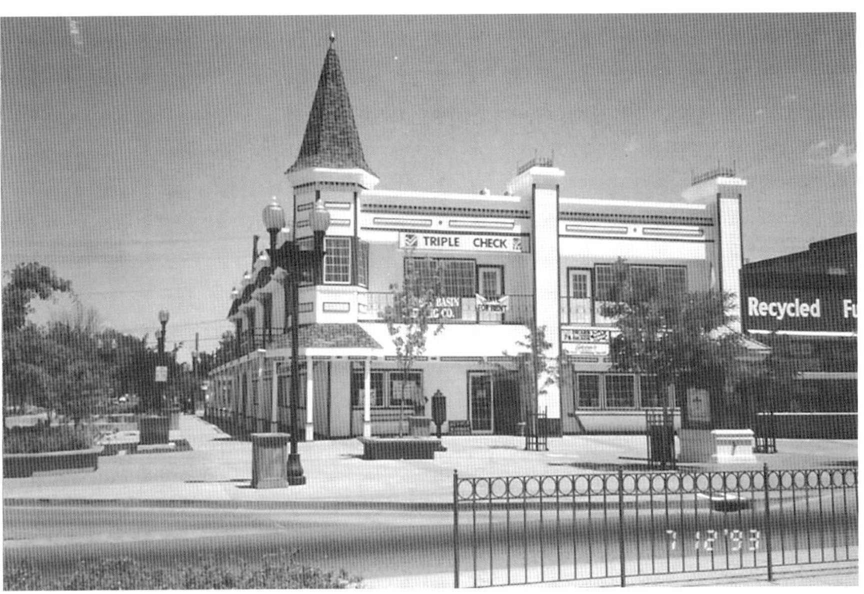

Great Basin Brewing Company's building following its renovation. *Courtesy Great Basin Brewing.*

Now on the search for a new location, discussions in downtown Reno led to a path of resistance, as the city was focused on casino development in the early 1990s. Sparks, however, was on board, as nothing else was happening in the city.

As the business plan was tailored to the new space, Young went to every bank imaginable in Nevada. Most liked the concept, but a geologist heading up a brewery didn't have any successful predecessors. Each investor who had earlier committed dropped out.

"When it comes to writing a check, things change," he said. "I made some more homebrew and set out to get new investors, and we raised some more money and I put every cent we had available into it. That's how entrepreneurs have to do it: chuck it all in and hope it works."

Young continued to run into problems throughout the construction process, with the physical construction and evolving bureaucracy with the city of Sparks, which had never seen a brewery before.

Great Basin Brewing was finally able to open in 1993, broke and desperate. The first night was a success and finished with a large stash of cash, which had no place to go since Young had forgotten to buy a safe. Instead, he stashed the thousands of dollars in a grain bag in the brewery.

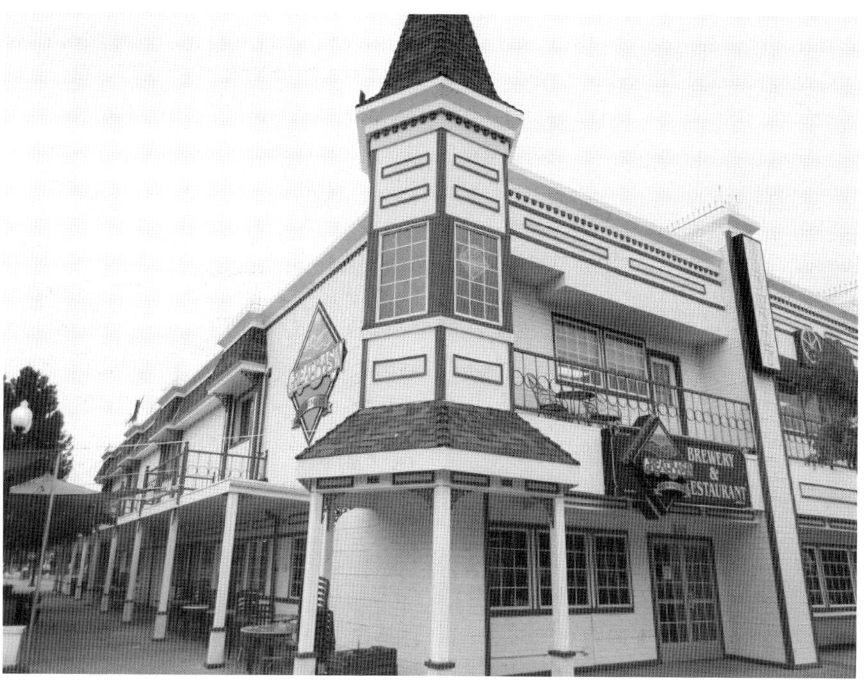

Great Basin Brewing Company's original location in downtown Sparks. *Courtesy Great Basin Brewing.*

"We hired staff, didn't train them," Young said. "We were looking around, we didn't think we were going to make payroll. We don't have the money to survive, so we open the doors. This was before cellphones, so I have no idea how anyone realized we were open and a brewpub, but it was packed, and good God did we need it.

"We had our beer, which was good. But good thing no one knew what a brewpub was and ordered food, because I found out why all those cooks didn't have jobs."

The Beer

Throughout the opening process, Young continued to brew beer. With the troubles of starting a brewery, he began chatting with another local award-winning homebrewer, Eric McClary. McClary had substantial financial backing from his parents and had never truly worked in his life, according to Young, so he asked him if McClary wanted a job brewing. McClary also ended up investing some money into the business.

In the months leading up to opening, Young took courses in fermentation sciences at UC-Davis and apprenticed, without pay, at four breweries in California and Arizona. He also spent money on a good new seven-barrel brewing system from JV Northwest.

Thanks to the homebrewing talent of McClary and Young, the opening beer portfolio of Great Basin Brewing had several award-winning beers. Since money limits only allowed for four fermenters in the original brewhouse purchase, the brewery opened with three flagship beers: Wild Horse Ale, an altbier that had won an American Homebrewers Competition; Nevada Gold, a kölsch; and Jackpot Porter. The fourth fermenter was saved for a Brewmaster's Special, the first of which went against the advice the bankers who didn't invest gave to Young to avoid aggressive beers: Ichthyosaur IPA.

The first seven-barrel batch of "Icky" IPA didn't last the first week. The bankers were wrong about the aggressive, hoppy and bitter beer. At the time,

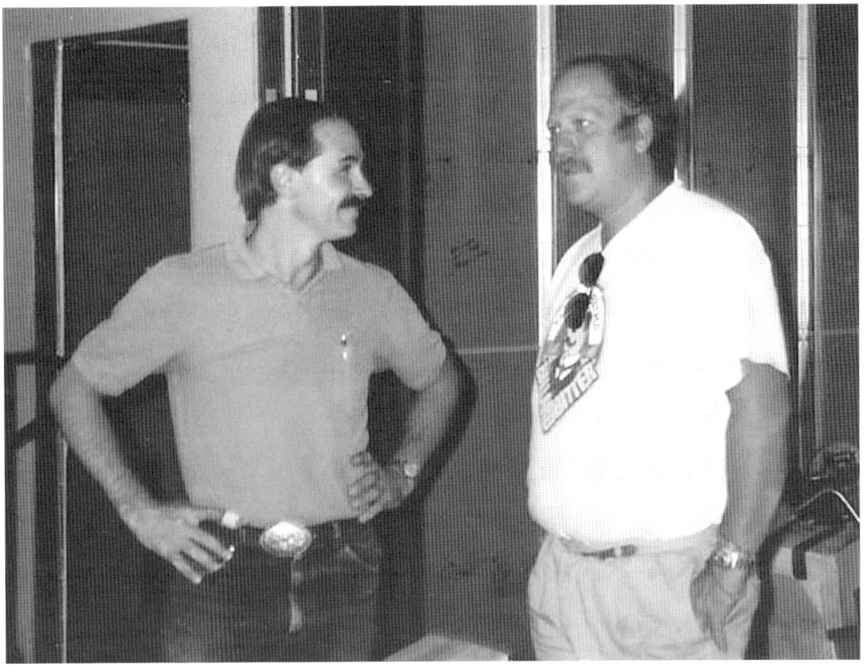

Great Basin Brewing founders Tom Young and Eric McClary chat at the brewery. *Courtesy Great Basin Brewing.*

Young believes it was one of the hoppier IPAs available on the West Coast of the United States, but in 2018, Young said he wouldn't even consider entering it into an IPA contest, as it barely meets the current standards.

"We still sell a lot of Icky," Young said. "It's changed some since we first brewed it, but now it pales in comparison to what is considered an IPA."

Nevada Gold is still brewed occasionally but was replaced in the full-time lineup with 39° North, a dry-hopped blonde ale, while Jackpot Porter was replaced with the oft-awarded Outlaw Milk Stout.

Great Basin Brewing is the most awarded brewery in Nevada, and the winning ways started early on with two Great American Beer Festival medals in its first year of competition: one for Wild Horse Ale and another for one of McClary's specialties, Cerveza Chilibeso.

The chili beer won gold medal all three years it was entered into GABF and has since been retired from competition. Young believes McClary was the first person to start using peppers in modern brewing, as he has been making the beer since the 1980s and winning homebrew competitions with the recipe. "It's unproven, so I don't know for sure, but he was very independent and wouldn't listen to anyone," Young said. Today, chili beer is its own category at the national competition.

"Eric was a lot more artistic than me, a really good artist with a film degree," Young said. "I would calculate hop bitterness and grain utilization ratios, and he'd say, 'Let's add some of this to round this out,' and that was the artist talking."

McClary is no longer with Great Basin Brewing, as he developed Parkinson's disease and eventually could no longer brew. He went back to Michigan with his wife and was last seen in a swimsuit near the river.

"His legacy lives on in so many of our beer styles," Young said.

EXPANDING GREAT BASIN

Once Great Basin opened its first taproom, it stayed popular for a bit before going through the normal growth curve of a restaurant, which slows down after an initial boom, Young said.

"We experienced that period, but we established ourselves and kept our finances together," he said. "The beer was good from the start, but we were a little worried that first year, but we figured out what we were doing, hired some better cooks and some of them are still forking for us today."

Before Great Basin Brewing's true brewpub reputation was known, the building would be packed starting at 2:30 p.m., seeing workers come stake out a table for when the rest of the people would show up at 5:00 p.m. The groups would have a beer or two, maybe some appetizers and move on by 7:00 p.m. To try to keep the crowd going, Young said Great Basin constantly held community events and became a hot spot for local bands.

While there was some excess capacity at points in the early years, allowing for some distribution for Great Basin Brewing, Young said it didn't take long for demand to meet the brewing capacity. Young was content to keep the small seven-barrel system going for several years before finally relenting and expanding the operation. Young said there was one year in the 1990s when the Sparks brewpub brewed nearly three thousand barrels of beer, all on the seven-barrel brewing system. "It was some innovative operations," Young said. "I'd get upset if a fermenter was free for two hours."

In 2010, Great Basin Brewing opened a second brewpub location, this time in Reno, which was capable of brewing another five to six thousand barrels of beer a year. With growth in mind, Great Basin Brewing quickly hit the upper limits of that capacity too. With the expansion into Reno, Great Basin finally had the capacity to make the journey to Las Vegas, where the brewery sees some success but is still limited by struggles with a tight market largely dictated by casinos and their clientele.

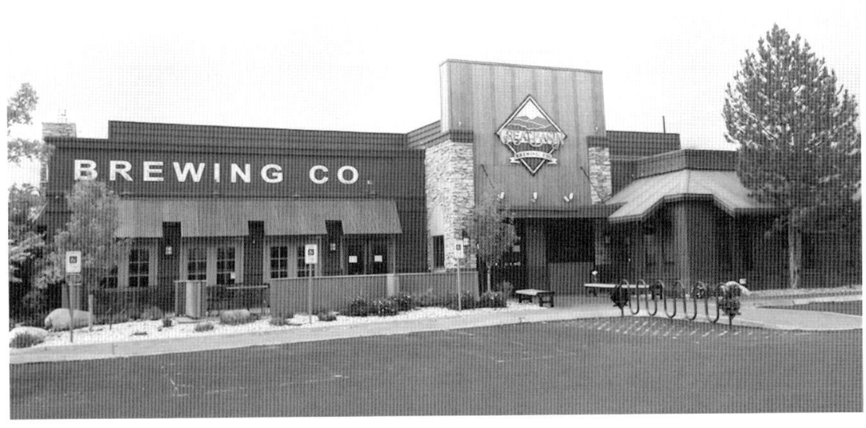

Great Basin Brewing Company opened its second taproom in Reno. The brewery makes beer at the original location, this location and a production facility. *Courtesy Great Basin Brewing.*

With a local production–minded brewery, Buckbean Brewing, going out of business in 2012, Great Basin Brewing took over the space and equipment with a full production facility in mind, and the Great Basin Taps and Tanks location opened.

"That was a tough road; the equipment was so bad," Young said. "It was all custom made, and for the time and money, that was probably a mistake. It probably would have been better to start from scratch."

With a full-blown production facility and plenty of room to grow, Great Basin Brewing brewed eleven thousand barrels of beer in 2017 and is distributed throughout Nevada, Northern California and Utah.

Great Basin's Winning Ways

While medals at beer competitions certainly don't mean everything, Great Basin has historically performed incredibly well at competitions, including the two major contests hosted by the Brewers Association.

Great American Beer Festival Medals
Cerveza Chilibeso: 1994 Gold, Herb and Spice
Wild Horse Ale: 1994 Bronze, Dusseldorf-Style Altbier
Wild Horse Ale: 1995 Bronze, Dusseldorf-Style Altbier
Cerveza Chilibeso: 1997 Gold, Herb/Spice Beers
Rye Patch Ale: 1998 Silver, Herb/Spice Beers
Cerveza Chilibeso: 1999 Gold, Herb and Spice Beers
Slam Dunkel: 2000 Silver, European-Style Dark/Munchner
Smoke Creek Rauchbier: 2006 Gold, Smoke-Flavored Beer
Wild Lemon Wheat: 2010 Bronze, Experimental Beer
Outlaw Oatmeal Stout: 2011 Bronze, Sweet Stout
Bitchin' Berry: 2013 Silver, Fruit Wheat Beer
Outlaw Milk Stout: 2014 Bronze, Sweet Stout or Cream Stout
The Great Pumpkin Ale: 2015 Bronze, Pumpkin Beer
Blood-Orange Wit: 2018 Silver, Belgian-Style Fruit Beer

World Beer Cup Medals
Slam Dunkel: 2002 Bronze, European-Style Dark/Munchner Dunkel
Death by Chocolate Stout: 2002 Gold, Chocolate/Cocoa-Flavored Beer
Black Rock ESB: 2002 Silver, Extra Special Strong Bitter

Outlaw Stout: 2008 Silver, Sweet Stout
Whoop Ass Witbier: 2010 Bronze, Belgian-Style Witbier
Outlaw Oatmeal Stout: 2012 Silver, Sweet Stout
Outlaw Milk Stout: 2014 Silver, Sweet Stout or Cream Stout
Truckee River Red: 2018 Bronze, American-Style Amber/Red Ale
Bitchin' Berry: 2018 Bronze, Fruit Wheat Beer

CHAPTER 11

BIG DOG'S BREWING (HOLY COW!)

I still have arguments with Kurt [Wiesner] *and Robert* [Snyder] *about who was first. It doesn't count; they closed and changed names.*
—Tom Young, founder of Great Basin Brewing in Reno

With Foxy's Firehouse casino closing on the Strip in 1988, a grandfathered non-restricted gaming license, allowing more than fifteen machines without five hundred required hotel rooms, was at risk of lapsing. A popular local businessman named Tom "Big Dog" Wiesner bought the building in 1989 with funds gained from selling the Marina Hotel, which still stands as the west wing of the MGM Grand. He reopened the casino as the Holy Cow! in 1992.

"It's hard to open a casino now; there's a high barrier of entry, so there's not a casino on every corner," said Robert Snyder, Big Dog's COO. "Imagine not having to build five hundred hotel rooms to open a casino; that would be pretty valuable to someone, and developers held that deal out to people and deal after deal fell through, until Tom came along and he had a bigger vision for the corner."

Holy Cow! opened without a brewery, but the plans were in the works from the very beginning. In 1992, there were 359 breweries in the United States, but as a beer-loving Wisconsin native, Wiesner felt like there was an opportunity for a brewery in Nevada, with freshly minted laws allowing brewpubs in the state. Like Tom Young in Reno, Wiesner was part of an important movement to help change the state law to allow for brewpubs in Nevada.

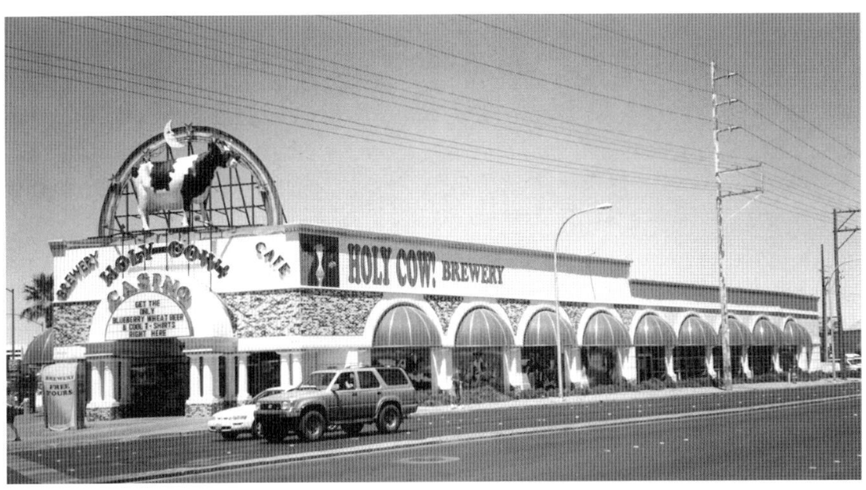

The Holy Cow! Casino and Brewery was the first brewery to open in Las Vegas. It closed in 2002, moved and changed names to Big Dog's Brewing. *Courtesy Nevada State Museum.*

Following the legislation allowing brewpubs, a 1998 *Las Vegas Review-Journal* article noted breweries began popping up like "discoteques in the '70s."

"I prefer microbrews," said airline pilot Dave Templin in the 1998 article that featured Big Dog's prominently. "I think they taste a lot better. I used to drink Coors, but not any more. When I buy beer at the store, I look for bottled microbrews."

The process was quick, accomplished fast to save the gaming license, Snyder said. The brewery had a ten-barrel system, and the beers were made on the second floor of the two-story building, with the bar on the first floor. The brewery opened with five beers: Holy Cow Pale Ale, Rebel Red Ale, Hefeweizen, Holy Cow Stout and Brewmaster's Special. The brewery would experiment with fruit extracts in the Hefeweizen. Original brewer Dan Rogers made a Witbier. One of the popular early seasonal beers was a pumpkin beer.

An IPA was made occasionally, but the style was yet to be ubiquitous with the craft beer movement at the time. "I would make IPA once every three months, and it wasn't a huge seller," said Dave Otto, who took over the brewery from Rogers in 1998. "We weren't even dry-hopping it then, which is hilarious—just a lot of late kettle hops. That was just the way people made IPAs back then."

Along with being sold at the casino on the Strip, Holy Cow's beers were sent to Big Dog Hospitality Group's seven restaurants across Las Vegas.

Those restaurants really only embraced the Pale, Red and Hefeweizen, according to Snyder.

Holy Cow! had a great deal for nearly ten years, and then a perfect storm struck. Shortly after September 11, 2001, Tom Wiesner was diagnosed with cancer and went to Seattle to fight it. He never returned, and his plans for a multimillion-dollar Chicago-themed resort disappeared.

"Think of the business environment in October 2001; it wasn't good and not appetizing for a guy who wanted to do a multimillion project," Snyder said. "He wanted that to happen, but he got sick, and the dreams of that project went away and that awesome real estate deal went away as well."

The landlord of the Holy Cow! building was set to raise the rent, and operating costs were set to rise $60,000 a month. Snyder said the profits to make up the difference were there with the margins at a brewpub and restaurant, and the decision to close the Holy Cow! came in 2002. Luckily, the brewery had a second life in store.

Big Dog's

Among his business empire, Tom Wiesner had opened Big Dog's Drafthouse. The plan was to move the brewery out to Big Dog's during the casino renovation, but the circumstances made the move a bit more somber. The move wasn't fluid, and the brewery closed for a period as the Drafthouse was renovated to accommodate the brewery, which also received a new fifteen-barrel brewhouse.

When the brewery reopened in 2003, the Drafthouse had been open for fifteen years and had a steady clientele. The ownership, now led by Tom Wiesner's son Kurt Wiesner, was worried the existing customers might shy away from the brewpub concept.

"We had people telling us to make it upscale and waiters in white shirts and ties," Snyder said. "We made the decision to keep it the same and casual and haven't looked back. We wanted to keep our people around; we were busy already and didn't want to piss that away."

With a house brewery, the company planned to make the transition to mostly house beers, so they decided to make a light beer called Leglifter Light to further entice the regular customers.

Likewise, a contest was held to rename the beers with dog-themed names in honor of Tom "Big Dog" Wiesner. "When the brewery opened, there was this intense desire to honor him," Snyder said. "One of the last things he said was, 'Get that thing built,' and the brewery was always his, but we started to consciously brand Big Dog's and the brewery together."

Beers changed. Rebel Red Ale became Red Hydrant. Holy Cow Pale Ale became Peace Love and Hoppiness. Holy Cow Stout became Black Lab Stout. Holy Cow Bavarian Hefeweizen became Tailwagger Wheat. The IPA was renamed Dirty Dog IPA and was made regularly. There also was Big Dog's Real Draught, supposedly a premium lager product meant to imitate Budweiser for the regulars, but it didn't sell well.

"People decide what you sell; we don't," Snyder said. "What's sold has changed over the years, and we sell a lot of hoppy beers. Our brewers have always embraced hoppy beers, and I think, at least around here, we were on the cutting edge of that."

The Big Dog's restaurants were slowly sold off and closed, but at its peak, Big Dog's sold 1,900 barrels of beer. Closing a location like Big Dog's on Sahara Avenue, which sold 300 barrels a year, in 2014 will put a dent in the overall barrelage, and it had to be recovered.

"We just beat that a couple years ago," Snyder said. "It's been very slow growth, and in hindsight, maybe we should have done it differently. Maybe

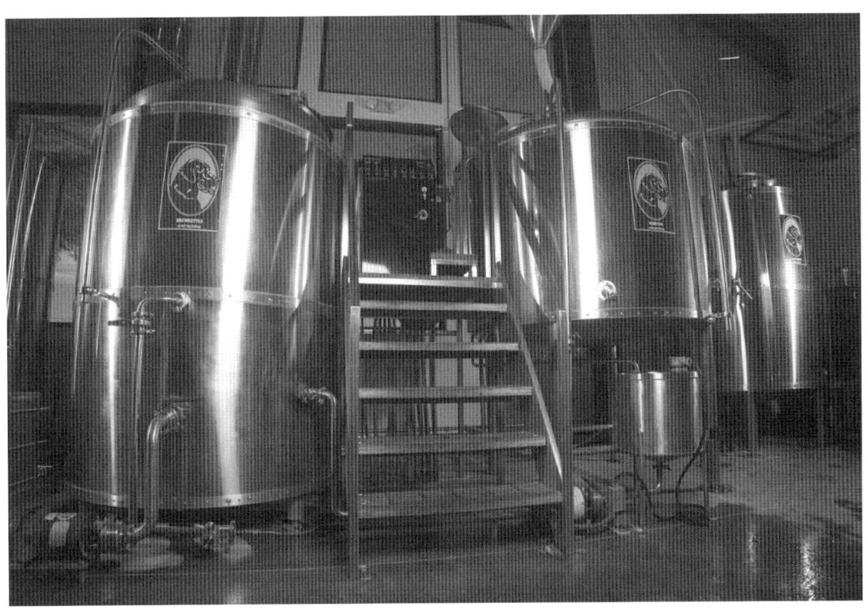

Big Dog's brewing system, which has made plenty of award-winning beer throughout the years the brewery has been open. *Courtesy Big Dog's Brewing.*

gone after the Strip back in the day; but there was no appetite for craft beer then."

There are plans for growth at Big Dog's Brewing. Behind the brewery, which is cramped and running close to capacity, are five acres of land owned by the company. Snyder said there are drawings for a production brewery on the land, along with an office building, with a beer park connecting the buildings.

Aside from the production facility, Snyder said there are no illusions to be anything bigger than a regional brewery. To help accomplish that goal, Snyder said there could be one or two satellite taprooms on the horizon. "Becoming a big, national craft brewery has left the station," Snyder said. "The answer is in taprooms and brewpubs where people interact directly with the product. I'd love to have a few tasting rooms along the Strip and higher-traffic tourist areas."

THE HOLY COW PROPERTY

Once the Holy Cow! Casino and Brewery closed in 2002, the building continued to live a fascinating life. The building and business's mascot, a fourteen-foot cow statue, was sold for $2,200 to Jim Marsh, a Nevada businessman who owned a slew of casinos and car dealerships in small Nevada towns, the largest being Tonopah. The cow made its way to Longstreet hotel-casino in Amargosa Valley, according to a 2005 *Las Vegas Review-Journal* profile on Marsh.

The building stood until it was demolished in 2012 after years of plans falling through.

In 2004, there was a $700 million, 940-foot-tall condominium project proposed by Australian Victor Altomare. A year later, Altomare was using the building as a sales office for another project, Liberty Tower, which also never got off the ground.

President Donald Trump's first wife, Ivana Trump, became involved with the building in 2005, when she associated with Altomare's original condo project called the Summit. The name was eventually changed to Ivana Las Vegas, as she decorated the building in pink. The project was soon cancelled.

In 2009, the *Las Vegas Sun* reported the property had been purchased for $47 million by Aspen Highlands Holdings LLC with plans for a new two-story building, including a Walgreens.

Big Dog's Brewers

Dan Rogers

Dan Rogers had been the chef at a Big Dog's Café, and when he learned Tom Wiesner wanted to open a brewery, he saw a future role. An avid homebrewer and bright man, Rogers would chat with Wiesner after work about beers, and according to Snyder, "all of a sudden, Dan was our brewer."

Rogers was sent to the Siebel Institute of Technology in Chicago to better learn the science of brewing.

After leaving Holy Cow! in 1998, Rogers continued his brewing career back in his home state of Michigan, first at Michigan Brewing Company, then at Big Rock Chop House and finally at Griffin Claw Brewing Company. His brewing skills never stopped growing, as he continued to be renowned in the beer-loving state of Michigan and his award-winning ways also continued.

At Michigan Brewing Company, Rogers won medals for No Disput'n Putin Russian Imperial Stout, Celis Grand Cru and two for Celis White.

While brewing at Big Rock Chop House & Brewery in 2010, Rogers won two medals—gold in American-style IPA and silver in Imperial IPA—for his Norm's Raggedy-Ass IPA and Bonnie's Raggedy-Ass Imperial IPA, respectively, both of which he still brews at Griffin Claw, which was opened by the Big Rock owners to showcase their beers. He also won Great American Beer Festival medals at Big Rock, including for Red Rock Belgian-style Lambic, Go Figure India Black Ale and American Brown Ale.

Griffin Claw won a silver medal in aged beer for its Oblivious Wheat Wine at the 2018 World Beer Cup.

Dave Otto

Dave Otto didn't intend to become a brewer. A longtime beer fan, Otto would drive to Washington, D.C., for monthly beer tastings in the early 1990s, when the East Coast was a relative beer desert. Sierra Nevada would show up to the bar with beers only available at its Chico, California brewery.

"Back then, it was even hard for us to get Sierra Nevada Pale Ale, so that was really cool for us to get those beers," Otto said. "When I would see the Pale Ale, I'd grab it and think it was some of the best beer I've ever had. A lot of these brewers coming up now, they've never even heard of some of these beers that I cherished back in the day because they're sort of irrelevant today."

The famed beer writer Michael Jackson would also come to the bar and regale the patrons with the history of some of the breweries offering up their beers.

Living in New Jersey at the time and being thirty years old with no real direction in life, Otto decided to move out to Las Vegas and go to the University of Nevada–Las Vegas. He frequented the Holy Cow! with Dan Rogers at the helm. He met Rogers one day while at a brewery under construction in Pahrump, when Otto recognized the Holy Cow! brewer wheeling in a branded keg. As they chatted, they learned a lot about each other, and Rogers eventually invited Otto to come get yeast and hops from the brewery.

"For a guy like me who was poor, going to school with no job, to save ten dollars was the biggest thing in the world," Otto said.

Each time he went to pick up ingredients, Otto would pop his head into the general manager's office and ask for a job. After countless nos, the general manager finally said, "Wait a minute, you want to be a slot host?" So Otto ended up taking care of customers at slot machines at the Holy Cow! until about six months later, when the assistant brewer put in his two weeks' notice. Rogers asked Otto if he'd be interested in the job. He was. The catch was he'd have to quit school, and the position paid a salary of $18,000—not great money in 1997. After a ninety-day probation, he was bumped up to $21,000.

Less than two years later, Rogers was headed back to Michigan and Otto was summoned to Tom Wiesner's office, where Wiesner told him that Rogers had recommended him for the head brewer position. "I said, 'Absolutely, there's no doubt in mind I can do it,'" Otto said. "Little did I know how much I didn't know back then, but I was confident I could do it."

Otto made the move with Holy Cow!'s brewing equipment after it closed on the Strip and was the head brewer at Big Dog's until 2015, when he left to help open PT's Brewing Company.

Otto now has more than twenty years of brewing experience in Las Vegas, a place he often thought about leaving. "But there's a lot to love about Vegas; that's probably why I never left," Otto said. "I love the weather, the cheap cost of living."

David Pascual

Like Otto, Big Dog's third head brewer made a mid-career switch after winning a number of awards at his previous brewery. For David Pascual, it was a move from Chicago Brewing in Summerlin to Big Dog's when Otto left.

Pascual started brewing in 2003 as a student at UNLV when he took a beer-tasting class as an upper-division elective. He excelled at the class and ended up interning at Barley's Casino & Brewery to satisfy a requirement for his biochemistry degree. His professor and Barley's head brewer Michael Ferguson offered him the internship.

Once he graduated, he heard Chicago Brewing was looking for an assistant and put his application for pharmacy school on the back burner. He figured a year at Chicago Brewing wouldn't harm any future career but ended up enjoying the work immensely.

"It was beer; how could you not love beer?" Pascual said. "For a while, my mom would ask me what my degree was in, and I would just tell her I thought I fell into something. Now my family is really proud."

With a whole cabinet of awards himself between Big Dog's and Chicago Brewing, Pascual is often asked how to become an award-winning brewer. "All I can say is I look and try other people's beers," he said. "What do I like and what can I emulate from other beers. Even mediocre beers I find something I like about."

His specialty came when his former boss at Chicago Brewing would brew up Belgian-style beers and Pascual would get headaches from them. He then started brewing them more, trying to understand where the connection was. "It made me question why I felt that way, and I'm not sure that was just immersing myself to drink them until I didn't get a headache, but it brought an appreciation," Pascual said. "It's my take on the classic styles, as true as I can be. They're so different—the spice, the fruit, the alcohol level, light to dark to sour to funky. It's the widest range of beers."

Under Pascual, the brewing team has continued to excel. The year before Pascual joined, Big Dog's brewed 1,700 barrels. His first year, they brewed 2,400 and added another 500 to the total in 2017.

"We're still young when it comes to growth," Pascual said. "The company is really pushing the beer and the brand. Sam [McKinney, director of packaging] has been here almost as long as I've been in the industry. Amanda [Koeller, lead brewer] is a UC-Davis graduate. It's a great team I was falling into. We're growing at a great rate, and we just need to keep an eye moving forward."

Big Dog's Winnings Ways

Great American Beer Festival Medals

Holy Cow! Pale Ale: 1993 Gold, Ale, Classic English Pale Ale
Holy Cow! Red Ale: 1994 Red Ale, English Brown Ale
Holy Cow! Stout: 1996 Bronze, Specialty Stouts
Holy Cow's Cream Ale: 2001 Silver, American-Style Lager/Ale or Cream Ale
Kilt Sniffer Strong Scotch Ale: 2006 Gold, Strong Scotch Ale
Alpha Dog Double Red Ale: 2008 Silver, Imperial or Double Red Ale
Belgian White: 2009 Silver, Belgian-Style Witbier
Red Hydrant Ale: 2012 Silver, English-Style Brown Ale
Red Hydrant Ale: 2015 Gold, English-Style Brown Ale
Tripel Dog Dare: 2016 Bronze, Belgian-Style Tripel
Tripel Dog Dare: 2017 Gold, Belgian-Style Tripel

World Beer Cup Medals

Holy Cow! Cream Ale: 2002 Silver, American Lager/Ale or Cream Ale
Holy Cow! Pilsner: 1998 Silver, Bohemian-Style Pilsener
Red Hydrant Ale: 2010 Gold, English-Style Brown Ale
Red Hydrant Ale: 2006 Gold, English-Style Brown Ale

CHAPTER 12

CASINOS BET ON BREWERIES

While casinos and the lively entertainment in Nevada are largely saddled with the slow adoption of craft beer in the state, the gaming establishments were some of the first and longest-operating breweries in the state. While the beers aren't the most innovative and likely won't capture the hearts of too many beer fans seeking the hot new brew, they get the job done. Casino breweries don't innovate and are extremely reminiscent of the beer menus most upstart breweries had in the early craft beer boom of the 1990s: pale, wheat, light lager, stout and amber, or some similar variation.

There's little reason to innovate for them, as these styles do plenty to satisfy their consumers. Still, it's an intriguing trend that took hold in the early craft beer wave, with many lasting well into the modern movement that has seen the nationwide brewery count blow by the pre-Prohibition high of more than 4,100 and into the 6,000s. For reference, there were 2,475 breweries in 2012 and more than 6,372 at the end of 2017.

The first casino brewery claims to be Brews Brothers at the Eldorado in Reno, which started operations in 1995. According to a 2002 *Reno Gazette-Journal* story, Brew Brothers ranked number one in brewpub production in 1998 and 1999.

Greg Hinge became the brewmaster of Brew Brothers in 2000, after several years of working under his friend and founding head brewer Darren Whitcher and earning his degree at the American Brewers Guild. In a tight space on the second floor of the casino, Hinge and another brewer make nearly 1,800 barrels of beer a year.

A set of six beers are always on tap, including the Big Dog IPA, Carano Extra, Redhead Amber Ale, Double Down Stout, Wild Card Wheat and Gold Dollar Pale.

In the craft-heavy Reno area, Hinge can't rest on his laurels and is regularly experimenting with two revolving Brewmaster Special tap handles. Hinge's Brew Brothers Barleywine won the bronze medal at the 2006 World Beer Cup, while Redhead Amber won gold the same year. In 2014, Brew Brothers took home bronze for Lou, a barrel-aged beer.

"We want to make fun beer and evolve with the scene," Hinge said. "For the mainstays, we do toy with them a bit, but we have our regular customers and they want to come in and know the Redhead Amber Ale is the same all the time."

Eldorado Resorts expanded the Brews Brothers concept with a facility in Columbus, Ohio, which opened in 2015.

In Las Vegas, several casinos felt the same trend in the 1990s and started breweries. Most are in off-the-strip casinos, likely as an attempt to draw more customers into their buildings.

In 1996, while in the midst of the first major wave of craft breweries in the United States, the Monte Carlo opened the Monte Carlo Pub & Brewery with brewmaster Erik Steiner at the helm. According to the *Las Vegas Sun*, the brewery opened with six beers, including a brewer's special. The five mainstays were a light beer, an IPA, an American-style unfiltered wheat ale, an Irish stout and an amber ale. All the beers were brewed on a twenty-barrel brewing system.

"We'll have a full range of tastes for all palates," Steiner told the *Sun*. "The Las Vegas Lite will be good for the heat, and we'll have brewers' special that change with the seasons. Our first special will be raspberry-wheat ale. In the summer we'll have a lot of fruit beers."

Steiner was a well-trained brewer, with studies at the American Brewers Guild, University of California and Temple University. He also worked at California's Black Diamond Brewing Company and Massachusetts Atlantic Coast Brewing prior to his arrival in Las Vegas.

The *Sun* described the atmosphere as "1910 urban East Coast warehouse," with a lot of copper pipes and a large bar and mirror. A pianist provided music for customers throughout the day, according to the article.

"Even if you're not a beer drinker, you'll enjoy visiting the Pub and Brewery," Stein said. "With our huge copper beer barrels and antique furnishings, it's an outstanding visual treat. The microbrewery will be one of the centerpieces of the property. It's one of the major draws into the Street of Dreams."

By all anecdotal accounts in 2018 by Las Vegas–area breweries and distributors, the property was a success and was among the highest-volume brewpubs in the nation. A 2000 article in the *Las Vegas Review-Journal* cited the Monte Carlo ranking number three nationally, brewing 108,000 gallons, or 3,484 barrels, in 1999, behind only a brewpub in Colorado and Brew Brothers in Reno. MGM Resorts International, which acquired the hotel in 2000 in a merger with Mirage Resorts, did not provide historical records pertaining to the brewpub.

The Monte Carlo brewpub closed in 2006 as the construction for Project CityCenter took over, a development that included the Aria, Mandarin Oriental and Vdara hotels.

MGM also had a brewpub in the New York New York Hotel & Casino.

Also opening in 1996 were Green Valley's Barley's Casino & Brewing Company—which was first a Gordon Biersch brewpub—in Henderson and Triple 7 Restaurant and Microbrewery at Main Street Station.

Triple 7 won Great American Beer Festival bronze and silver for its Black Cherry Stout in 1999 and 1997, respectively. Barley's won a bronze medal for its Black Mountain, a European-style dark, in 2005 and silvers for Barley's Would Gold Hefeweizen and Brewmaster Select Hefeweizen in 2002 and 2000, respectively. Triple 7 still serves up Black Cherry Stout as one of its Brewmaster's Specials, along with a year-round lineup of High Roller Gold, Double Down Hefeweizen, Marker Pale Ale, Royal Red and Black Chip Porter. In 2018, Triple 7 released a collaboration beer with San Diego's Stone Brewing Company, Eh, Waddyagunnado, an 8 percent ABV double red ale, with loads of tropical hops from New Zealand and the Pacific Northwest.

Barley's serves up a standard rotation of four beers—the Blue Diamond German Helles, Black Mountain dark lager, Red Rock Oktoberfest and Boulder Gold Hefeweizen—along with a seasonal and Brewmaster's Special tap.

In 2017, Barley's handed control of its brewery to those at Banger Brewing from downtown Las Vegas in an effort to expand the Henderson operation's clientele, according to an article in the *Las Vegas Review-Journal*. "The craft beer crowd doesn't necessarily correlate with a casino," Barley's general manager Jonathan Veltri told the *Review-Journal*. "We're trying to bring both of those together."

In 1998, Ellis Island launched its brewery and became the Ellis Island Hotel, Casino & Brewery. Dating back to 1968, Frank Ellis started a local restaurant called the Village Pub on Koval Avenue, east of the Strip. He sold the restaurant to his son Gary Ellis in 1985. He changed the name to Ellis Island, added a casino in 1989 and, almost a decade later, added the brewery in a renovation project.

Longtime brewing professional Joe Pickett has led the brewery, which touts itself as the number-one brewery in Las Vegas and often sells its beers for less than two dollars. In his brewing, Pickett aims to brew beers with mass appeal rather than the limited market of craft beer enthusiasts, and Ellis Island brews more than two thousand barrels of beer a year, limited to a small lineup including light, amber, Weiss, stout and English-style IPA, as well as seasonal specialties like hard root beer, hard lemonade, Oktoberfest, Winter Spiced Ale and Red Irish Ale.

Ellis Island is doubling down on its commitment to the brewing industry and started a $10 million expansion project in 2017 with a two-story addition called the Front Yard, with a "casual brewpub atmosphere, bar games and activities, regular live entertainment and a dazzling neon view of the Las Vegas Strip," according to a release from the company.

"Ellis Island has been a Las Vegas destination for generations," said Christina Ellis, the company's director of marketing. "The Front Yard is an exciting addition to the property that will offer something new and engaging to our guests while retaining the inviting, family-oriented feeling that Ellis Island is known for."

In a town full of casinos and mega-resorts, only a select few took on the endeavor to make their own beer. It took many others decades to even catch on to the growing trend of locally brewed and craft beer, a reputation that hurts the city's beer culture image nationally well into 2018.

PART V

CRAFT CULTURE

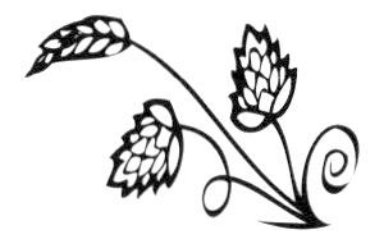

CHAPTER 13

LAS VEGAS

Tenaya Creek

Tim Etter and his three siblings, all Las Vegas natives, launched Tenaya Creek Brewery in 1999. Tim began homebrewing when his roommate at the University of Utah introduced it to him, ended up heading to the fermentation sciences program at UC-Davis and later honed his brewing abilities at Uinta Brewing in Utah.

In 2008, Tenaya Creek doubled down on the focus of beer, nixed the food service part of the business and launched its beer into distribution. By 2010 and again in 2014, the company had to expand its beer production capabilities.

Anthony Gibson is the head brewer at Tenaya Creek and first became interested in beer when he visited Tim Etter at Uinta Brewing—before the Etter family opened Tenaya Creek in 1999. "When I saw what he was doing, I really just got an early idea of what it meant to be a brewer," Gibson told *Vegas Seven* in 2013.

In 2015, Tenaya Creek made a move from its original location on North Tenaya Way to Bonanza Road in downtown Las Vegas. Tim Etter invested $1 million into the new space, which was once a plumbing supplies building. The move was necessitated by a need for more space to increase the brewing ability, Tenaya Creek sales manager Alex Graham told *Vegas Seven* in 2015. According to a 2015 *Las Vegas Review-Journal* article, the original location had a capacity two thousand barrels a year, while the new space could brew up to six thousand barrels annually.

"We have not reached full capacity, but we don't want to get stuck in that situation," Graham said.

The new facility allowed Tenaya Creek to start canning its beers and provided a large cooler for packaged beers heading to distribution and eight new fermenters, as well as a more brewery- and beer-focused taproom—without gaming or smoke.

"The taproom has such a different feel from our other bar," Gibson said on a TenayaCreek.com blog post. "Our guests constantly comment how comfortable and inviting our taproom is and how great the beer selection is. It has the feeling of being in another city because of the absence of gaming machines and smoking."

As the old equipment was left in the original Tenaya Creek building, the move allowed for a turnkey operation for an aspiring brewery, an opportunity taken by Golden Entertainment to launch PT's Brewing.

Now well settled into the new facility, Tenaya Creek's beers are making their way further into the beer drinker's mind, including beers like Hop Ride IPA, Bonanza Brown Ale, Craft Pilsner, 702 Pale Ale, Gypsy Fade IPA and Hauling Oats Oatmeal Stout.

Tenaya Creek won a 2014 bronze for Bonanza Brown Ale and a 2002 gold for Tenaya Creek Pilsner at the Great American Beer Festival.

Sin City Brewing

Growing up, Richard Johnson had no intention of becoming a brewer. His college years were in the mid-1980s, when craft beer began to poke its head out of the water. Johnson wasn't paying attention. He'd occasionally choke down an import like Guinness or Bass, but domestic light lagers dominated the market. His view of beer changed when he traveled to Europe while in college, as it did with so many brewers in that generation.

He flew into London. He biked ten days to Wales for a ferry to Ireland. On his ride, he'd stop at pubs dotted across England. "Their world hadn't gone through the same consolidation," Johnson said. "They still had all these traditional breweries, and these great old beers were still around."

He wasn't a beer fan yet, but being young and experimental, tasting new flavors, he decided to journal his trip. He still has the beer journal. He'd make up stories about the beers and their flavors. He'd draw the pubs, an entirely different atmosphere than the bars in America. The beer culture in England changed his perception of what could be. In Ireland, beer culture was Guinness culture, further evolving his idea of the ancient beverage. "In Ireland, Guinness is an everyday drink," he said. "We thought of it as an occasional beer, and that changed my whole entire attitude of what beer could be."

On his return from Europe, he worked for airlines. The job entitled him to cheap travel, a privilege he used to further his horizons and learn more about beer. He spent a lot of time in Germany. While England and Ireland were ale cultures, Germany had a love of lagers, styles of beer marginalized in America with the dominance of macro light lagers. "The big breweries in Germany were making incredible beers, not just because they were brewing them for hundreds of years, but because they didn't dumb them down," Johnson said. "They made flavorful, interesting lagers."

For whatever reason, beer struck Johnson in the right spot, and throughout college, he and his friend would have beer night on Thursdays, bringing beers they made and discovered to share, and according to him, they would "pretend to talk about them like we knew what we were talking about."

Looking back now, he recalls most of the beers were terrible, but the social aspect was the major draw, and he particularly liked the science of the beer, the history behind it and the artistic expression of the labels. With the interest well embedded, by the time brewpubs began popping up across the United States in the late 1980s, he was old enough to work in them. Most people would lean to bartending, a quite lucrative career if done well and in a successful bar, but Johnson leaned toward brewing.

"I always liked to make things; I've always been creative," he said. "We always did things with our hands; it was important to my dad. And to me, making beer was more interesting than selling beer."

He took what he called the "vow of poverty" in a life of brewing, a laborious and tedious career, often short on pay. In 1989, he knew the brewer at the original Gordon Biersch brewpub in Palo Alto, California, and latched on to the new-age lager brewery.

"At the time, it was kind of an avant-garde lager brewery. At the time, no one in the craft space was making lagers, and these were so different from the macro lagers," Johnson said. "People didn't know how to take them because these beers were aggressive compared to what was available. They made four lagers that were blowing the minds of domestic beer fans, and looking back now, they're all approachable."

Knowing a brewer at Gordon Biersch, Johnson learned that the company was looking for a second brewer at its second location, and he took an internship. He saw Dan Gordon, one of the founders, and saw the brewing doctorate earned in Munich, Germany, as an asset he could learn from. In the 1980s, there was no real homebrewing subculture, according to Johnson. There was no Internet to learn from, no books widely available. This was his chance to have a real mentor and learn crucial information if he were to have a brewing career.

Johnson said Gordon was a very different brewer than most of his contemporary beer entrepreneurs, buttoned-up and strict in traditional German brewing, as opposed to the "hippie brewers." "It wasn't lax; it was structured and disciplined," Johnson said. "I was that hippie guy, but it changed my whole process."

As a brewer, he worked five days a week, brewing, cleaning, transferring and multitasking, for two years.

While he cherished the opportunity, a company in Whistler, British Columbia, approached him about working in its lager brewery. There, another Bavarian brewer with similar strict brewing tendencies was in charge. "I was getting pigeonholed in that Bavarian thing," Johnson said.

Following two years in Canada, he went back to Gordon Biersch, which was getting ready to enter Southern California with new breweries. Johnson figured he'd make himself valuable and started installing and training brewers at the new locations, first in Southern California and then in Hawaii, and eventually it became his gig as the company continued to expand. "That was really cool, because I got to travel and learn new things," he said. "I'd go from production to construction to training and back and forth. It was an incredible experience with a growing company."

By the time he left Gordon Biersch, he was stationed in Las Vegas and running fifteen breweries on the West Coast.

He started to get an itch more than a decade into his career with Gordon Biersch. He was growing older, and in his mid-forties, the next career move would be either lateral or entrepreneurial. "In your mid-forties, something starts to click, not a panic, but a biological pipeline, and I started asking myself, 'Is this my life?'" he said.

Even though he had been dragged to Las Vegas "kicking and screaming," Johnson saw his future in southern Nevada. He had his family here, after all. With a stake in Las Vegas and an idea with a few friends for a business, he saw an opportunity on the Strip.

"There was no craft beer in casinos, no local beers," he said. "As far as interesting beers, there was Sam Adams, Sierra Nevada and, oddly enough, Newcastle."

He started Sin City Brewing Company in 2003 with the intention of making it the Strip's brewery. His model wasn't production minded; in fact, he would brew the beers at other breweries—first at Gordon Biersch in Las Vegas and now at Lovelady Brewing, owned by his former co-worker Richard Lovelady. Instead, he wanted to be a taproom model, utilizing taprooms he believes are like the ones he remembers from his trips to Europe as a student. He tries to find partnerships on the Strip that make sense and has been turned off at times by the way some of the casino properties treat their beer. In 2018, there are four Sin City Brewing locations, with a flagship taproom on Harmon Corner.

At Gordon Biersch, Johnson's job wasn't just about making good beer but reproducing good beer. While breweries across the country—most of the more than six thousand in business—focus on beer innovation, Johnson sticks to what he knows. "My focus has been brewing traditional styles and loving the fact that these beers have been around for hundreds of years and paying homage to them and obeying their styles," he said.

The lineup at Sin City Brewing Company is simple: Weisse, blonde, amber, IPA and stout, with a few seasonal beers. His philosophy explains

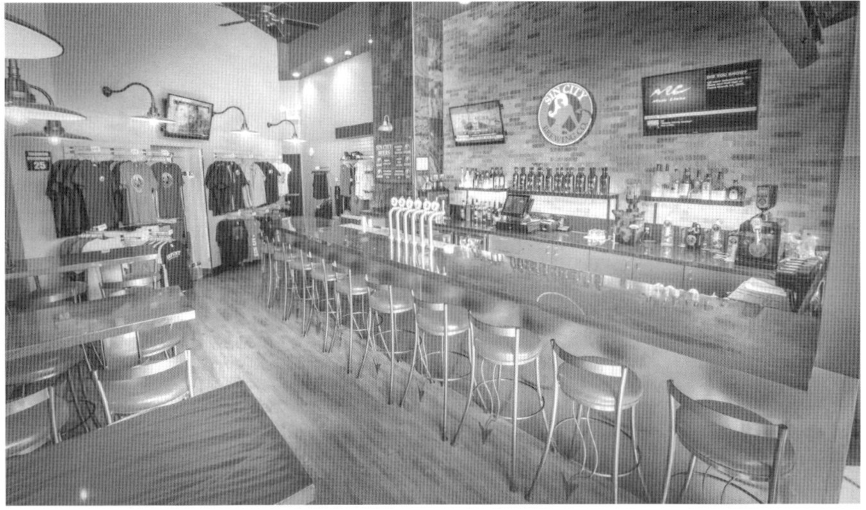

The interior of Sin City Brewing's flagship location on Harmon Corner on the Strip. *Courtesy Sin City Brewing.*

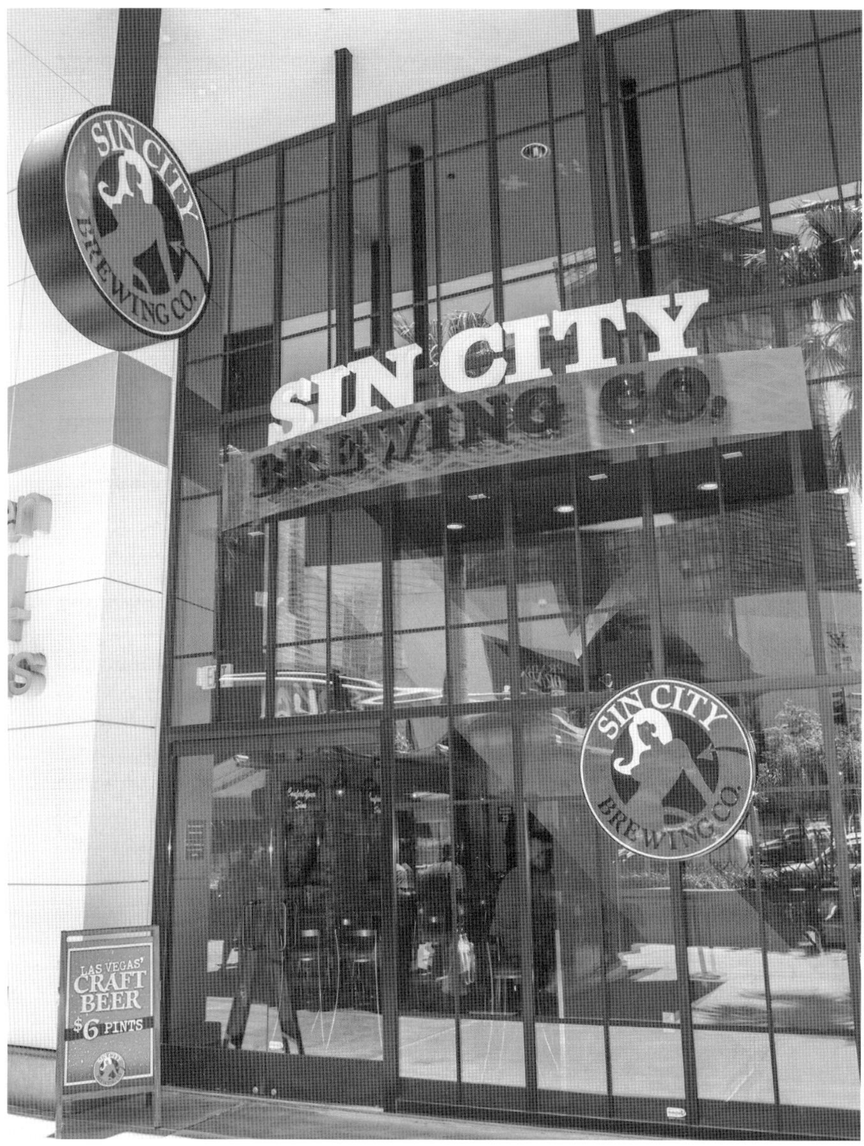

Above: The flagship location of Sin City Brewing, located on the corner of Harmon Corner. *Courtesy Sin City Brewing.*

Opposite, top: Sin City Brewing's Grand Canal Shoppes location at the Venetian. It opened in 2009; *Opposite, middle*: Sin City Brewing's Miracle Mile Shops, a 475,000-square-foot retail complex in Planet Hollywood on Las Vegas Boulevard; *Opposite, bottom*: Sin City Brewing's Grand Bazaar Shops locations at Bally's on Las Vegas Boulevard. *Courtesy Sin City Brewing.*

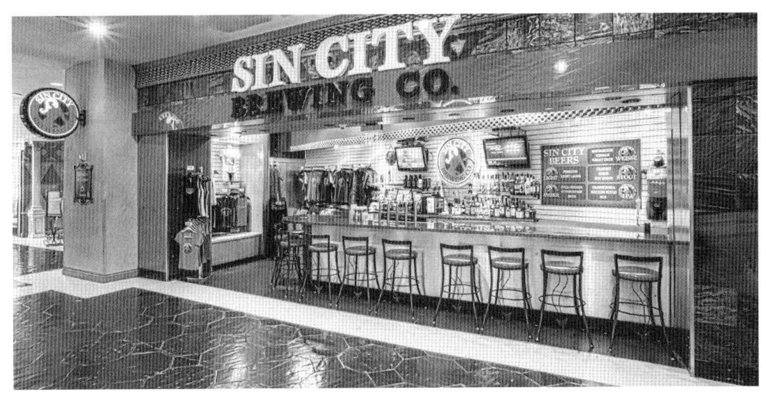
SIN CITY
BREWING CO.
SIN CITY BEERS

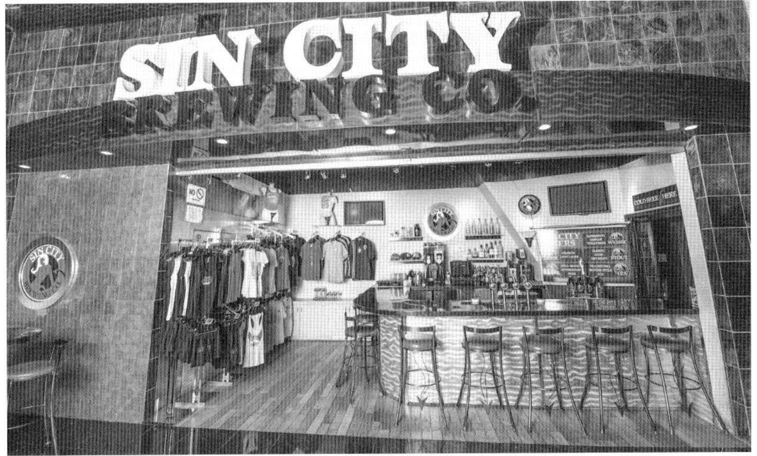
SIN CITY
BREWING CO.

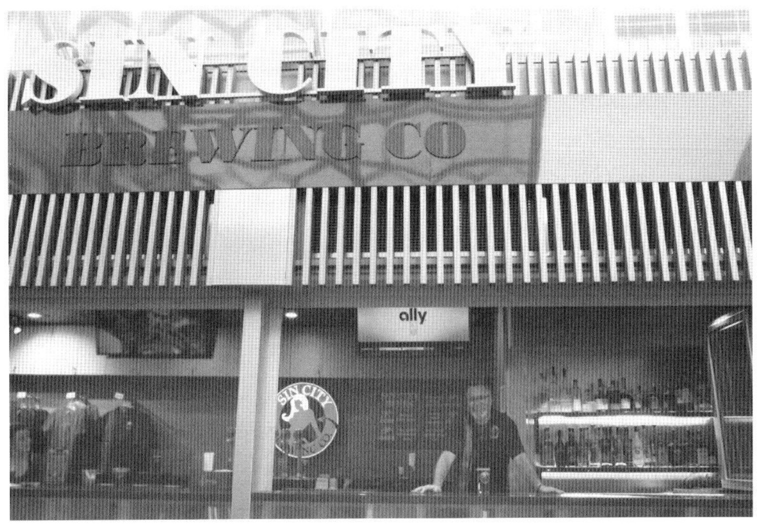
SIN CITY
BREWING CO
ally

the simplicity and why his IPA is more in line with an English-style IPA than West Coast IPA or even the trendy Northeast IPA. "I love what they're doing today," he said of other breweries. "But I wish there was a better way to talk about what those beers are."

So with several Sin City Brewing taprooms stretched along the Strip and well into a thirty-year career in brewing, Johnson has found his spot, a company that shares his identity. "I work with people I like and make beer I want," he said. "I'm happy with where we are, and we try to grow a bar every two years. We recognize limitations on the Strip as far as culture, but I think beer travelers have evolved where they want local products no matter where they go. We're not San Diego, but we have great beer in this town."

Banger Brewing

With a grain silo and big sign on the exterior of its retail space, Banger Brewing helps welcome visitors to the covered stretch of Fremont Street, a must-see in Las Vegas for locals and tourists alike.

Five friends, all of whom met in high school or at restaurants within the Bellagio, came together to open the brewery in December 2013. Spearheaded by Michael "Banger" Beaman, who brews up the beer, the group first looked into real estate before falling into beer in 2010.

Beaman would brew up beer for the group's camping trips, and the homebrews would show up at local beer festivals. Eventually, the draw into the industry was simply too much. Beaman is joined in the venture by Nick Fischella, Eddie Quiogue, Marc Longwith and Robert Mendoza.

Next to Heart Attack Grill, the three-thousand-square-foot retail space is a small taproom and brewery but plenty big enough to make it a tantalizing stop for visitors to Fremont Street. The brewery sits in the shopping mall Neonopolis, just east of the covered Fremont Street Experience.

"It's a lost block, like the 38th parallel," Longwith told the *Review-Journal* in 2013, prior to opening. "There's 2 million locals on East Fremont and 16 million tourists under the canopy. They never mix. We're hoping to bridge that gap."

The quintet was able to buy a brewing license for $7,500, thanks to a Las Vegas ordinance that passed in 2013; otherwise they would have faced a steep $75,000 liquor license for full bar service. The partners were also helped along by investor Tony Hsieh, the top dog at Zappos and a big proponent of a strong Las Vegas downtown.

With not a lot of space to work with, Banger opened with a three-barrel brewhouse and five seven-barrel fermenters.

El Heffe, a jalapeño-infused hefeweizen, has become a familiar sight around Las Vegas. Banger's other year-round beers are Perfect Ten American Pale Ale, DTB Brown Ale, Morning Joe Coffee Kölsch and Hop Culture Reference, an IPA made with a single rotating hop. Seasonal releases include Hop Bang Boom Imperial IPA, Sandia Watermelon Wheat, Rebellion Red and Spring Training, a grapefruit-infused saison. Beaman also experiments with barrels stored around the small taproom, ranging from bourbon barrels to gin barrels.

In 2017, Barley's Casino & Brewing Company in Henderson partnered with Banger to help further the longtime casino operation's brewing reputation. It started as a contract-brewing relationship, with Banger Brewing at Barley's, but blossomed into more. "A lot of people don't even know Stations has a brewery," Barley's general manager Jonathan Veltri told the *Las Vegas Review-Journal* in 2017. "We're trying to rebrand the name. The craft beer crowd doesn't necessarily correlate with a casino. We're trying to bring both of those together."

Banger isn't the only brewery with a presence on this entertaining stretch of glitz and glamor. Chicago Brewing, which is truly located out in Summerlin, has a location in the Four Queens Hotel and Casino on Fremont Street. Triple 7 Restaurant and Microbrewery is also nearby on Main Street.

HOP NUTS

As for most craft beer fans and modern brewers, hops are at Kevin Holder's heart—hence the name of his brewery, Hop Nuts Brewing, which opened in downtown Las Vegas's Arts District in 2015.

Holder was born in California but moved to Las Vegas in 1992, graduating from high school and UNLV before ending up as an MRI technician in Las Vegas. He worked nearly nonstop for seven years to make his dream of owning a brewery and working for himself a reality. Once the brewery was open, he quit his medical jobs and made his full-time career in the brewhouse.

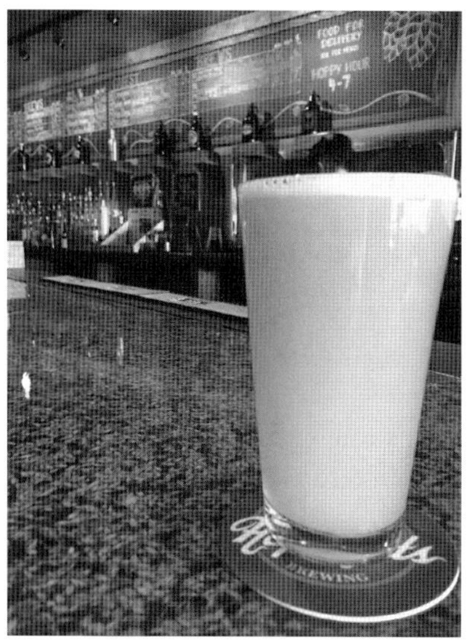

A hazy IPA sits on the bar at Hop Nuts Brewing in downtown Las Vegas. Hop Nuts owner Kevin Holder likes brewing hop-forward beers. *Photo by Pat Evans.*

"I really like what's going on in the Downtown area," Holder told *Las Vegas Weekly* in 2015. "I want to be part of the neighborhood I grew up in, where I rode my bicycle as a kid. To have my own business here is a trip."

While Hop Nuts plays to his love of hops, the brewery's main lineup is full of IPAs, double IPAs and pale ales, but it's also been a less hoppy beer to make waves for the brewery. As the NHL's Vegas Golden Knights announced their name in November 2016, Holder realized he had the perfect name for his previously unnamed golden strong ale: Golden Knight. The Golden Knight is a light-body Belgian-style strong ale with a sweet but dry finish, an easy drinker for the relatively high 7.5 percent ABV. The Golden Knight became a star during pregame festivities outside T-Mobile Arena, where the Golden Knights play their home games, in the team's inaugural season, in which they became the first expansion franchise to reach the Stanley Cup finals since the St. Louis Blues in 1968.

In 2018, Hop Nuts began canning beers from its lineup, including the Golden Knight. Other beers brewed by Hop Nuts include 18b Pale Ale, with Azacca, Simcoe and Cascade hops; Hopathon IPA, with loads of tropical and pine flavors; and Green Mamba Double IPA, a big West Coast double IPA with more than 100 IBUs, a beer Holder says is for "Hop Nuts only."

Along with the hop bombs and the Golden Knight, Holder also likes to brew a variety of other lighter Belgian-style beers, like a Belgian wit and a light golden ale.

Chicago Brewing

Chicago Brewing started up in early 2000 and was featured in a 2000 *Las Vegas Review-Journal* piece announcing its opening, along with Tenaya

Creek Brewing's opening in late 1999. Even in 2000, it was noted that the Las Vegas brewing scene lagged behind much of the rest of the nation. America had 1,566 breweries in 2000, and Las Vegas, then a city of 1.3 million, had 10.

Much of the rest of the United States started to experience a surge following a dramatic slowdown and dip of breweries in the late 1990s. With Chicago Brewing and Tenaya Creek, it appeared Nevada might follow. Even those at the companies realized brewing in Nevada at the time was a tad slow, it wasn't really until another dozen or so years that the trend fully took hold as the nation grew exponentially.

The then general manager of Tenaya Creek told the *Review-Journal*, "The microbrew trend hit here relatively late" and credited the surge to people moving to Las Vegas with a taste for better beer. At the time, craft beers only accounted for approximately 4 percent of beer consumed in America, a number that increased to 12.7 percent by 2017.

According to the *Las Vegas Sun*'s short description of Chicago Brewing in its directory, "themed venues were all the rage in the late '90s, and this brewery and restaurant aimed to fill the Windy City void."

While the brewery doesn't make much beer—fewer than one thousand barrels each year as of 2017—it is nearing its capacity, head brewer Kyle Cormier said in a 2017 *Las Vegas Review-Journal* story.

Chicago Brewing also opened a brewpub in the Four Queens hotel in downtown Las Vegas.

David Pascual, now the director of brewing operations at Big Dog's Brewing, started his full-time brewing career as an assistant brewer at Chicago Brewing in 2005. "I loved that place," Pascual said of Chicago Brewing. "I still know that place like the back of my hand. It was a next step sort of thing, because I didn't know where they wanted to grow the brand and I wanted to push myself and get out of my comfort zone." He became the brewery's head brewer in 2008 before leaving for Big Dog's in 2015.

Chicago Brewing's lineup of beers includes All Nighter, a blonde ale with light floral notes; Weizenheimer, a German-style wheat with clover and banana esters; Ramblin Reck Amber, an amber ale with caramel maltiness and piney hops; Old Town Brown, a brown ale with toffee nuttiness; Sun Down Stout; and Hardway IPA.

Great American Beer Festival Medals
Old Town Brown: 2002 Silver, German-Style Brown Ale
Daisy Chain: 2002 Silver, Belgian-Style Abbey Ale
Vienna Lager: 2004 Gold, Golden or Blonde Ale
CBC Ultimate Weiss: 2004 Gold, German-Style Wheat Ale
All Nighter: 2005 Bronze, Golden or Blonde Ale
Weizenbock: 2005 Silver, German-Style Wheat Ale
Hawaiian Honey: 2007 Bronze, Specialty Honey Lager or Ale
All Nighter: 2008 Bronze, Golden or Blonde Ale
Wild-Westmalle Tripel: 2011 Silver, Belgian-Style Tripel
Cocoa for Coconuts: 2012 Gold, Chocolate Beer
Quad Damn It: 2013 Silver, Belgian-Style Strong Specialty Ale
Wild West Tripel: 2015 Gold, Belgian-Style Tripel
Quad Damn It: 2015 Bronze, Belgian-Style Strong Specialty Ale

World Beer Cup Medals
Daisy Chain: 2004 Bronze, Belgian-Style Tripel
C.B.C. Belgian-Style Dubbel: 2006 Gold, Belgian-Style Tripel
Daisy Chain Tripel: 2010 Gold, Belgian-Style Tripel
Mad Monk Dubbel: 2010 Silver, Belgian-Style Dubbel

PT's Playground

PT's Brewing Company launched in early 2016 with the intended goal of supplying its growing collection of taverns with beer. Parent company Golden Entertainment purchased Tenaya Creek Brewery's original location on Las Vegas's west side, and PT's quickly became one of the state's most widely distributed beers simply because of the company's more than fifty taverns in the region.

"Craft beer is a growing business in the Las Vegas Valley, and our PT's Brewing Company has quickly made its own mark as a compelling new entry into this market," PT's Entertainment Group director of tavern operations Brent Edlund told *Las Vegas Weekly* in March 2017. "Our growing operations offer the brewery the perfect platform to introduce our handcrafted beers to a new audience."

PT's set out to launch with some of the best beer in the Las Vegas Valley and tapped longtime area brewer Dave Otto, the award-winning talent from

Big Dog's. Otto was looking for a new career challenge at the time and agreed to make the jump. Otto kept his winning ways as he started brewing at PT's, winning a bronze medal at the 2017 Great American Beer Festival for Boulder Stout.

Along with Boulder Stout, PT's makes a variety of beers, but only four really make their way to the other taverns, meaning a visit to the PT's Brewing Company taproom involves some specialty brews. The three other beers distributed to other taverns in 2017 include Hualapai IPA, Sean Patrick's Irish Red and Golden Hefeweizen.

By early 2018, PT's Brewing was already nearing capacity at the old Tenaya Creek brewery, making nearly three thousand barrels of beer. This limited the creativity Otto had to play with in brewing and necessitated constant brewing of the flagship brews needed to supply the taverns. Early on in the brewery's existence, Otto joked to the *Las Vegas Review-Journal* in March 2016 that his plan was to "get this thing up and running, max it out and force the company to build me a bigger brewery."

PT's Brewing was easy to get off the ground in a preexisting facility with a ten-barrel barrel brewhouse and an array of fermenters ranging from fifteen barrels to forty barrels. At the time of publication, PT's Brewing didn't have any official plans for expansion, but talks were ongoing.

BOOZE DISTRICT

An industrial park off Eastgate Road was christened the Artisan Booze District in 2013, when Las Vegas Distillery, Grape Expectations, Nevada School of Winemaking and CraftHaus Brewery decided to team up for the label. CraftHaus was still a year from opening.

A distribution conundrum for Las Vegas Distillery led to the creation and location of Booze Brothers Distributing in the same space as Las Vegas Distillery. Before long, Bad Beat Brewing joined the district.

The park's developer was open to the idea, and the entire area was rezoned to allow for retail sales as well.

"We realize the value that each of these businesses brings to Henderson," Henderson mayor Andy Hafen told the *Las Vegas Review-Journal* in 2015. "The hundreds of small businesses in our community are a big part of the lifeblood of our city. These companies contribute to the growth of our local economy and help keep valuable dollars and jobs in our community."

Hungarian George Racz came to Henderson with the idea of making booze and distilled his first whiskey in 2011, when the state legalized distilling thanks to a bill written by Racz. With the rezoning of the district, Racz was able to open a whiskey and spirits bar in 2015. Likewise, Grape Expectations opened the Vegas Valley Winery.

As for the breweries, Bad Beat Brewing was able to open its doors first, followed by CraftHaus Brewery.

There are no signs of the Artisan Booze District slowing. Astronomy Aleworks opened in 2018, with a theme centered on science fiction, astronomy and astrophysics.

CraftHaus Brewery

As with many other small brewery owners, Wyndee and Dave Forrest first fell in love with beer in Europe. The newfound passion led into a crazy journey of eventual entrepreneurship, but few other journeys potentially changed the direction of a region's beer industry like the path CraftHaus Brewery traversed.

Following their graduation from UNLV in 2004, Wyndee and Dave decided to take a trip to Europe. While in Amsterdam, a server brought the couple beers. "There was rainbows and unicorns, and it opened our eyes, yes, to the full flavor," Wyndee said, "but most of all that it brought people together."

Through the rest of their European travels, the couple sought out beer, especially in beer-centric regions like Bavaria, stopping at every tiny brewery they could find.

Back home in southern Nevada, the Forrests couldn't find beer that satisfied their newfound taste buds. Tenaya Creek Brewery and Big Dog's were up and well established, but in the sprawl, the cross-town journey from Henderson was daunting. Instead, Dave started homebrewing and quickly took over the house.

Four years into brewing, Sierra Nevada Brewing put out a call for submissions to attend its annual Beer Camp. The craft beer pioneer chose ten winners from across the country, including Dave Forrest, who was able to spend three days brewing and chatting with Ken Grossman, one of the pillars of the modern beer industry.

"He comes back and said, 'We need to move to Chico,'" Wyndee said. "Instead, let's make our own version for our community and craft beer scene."

The couple spent another four years planning the brewery, reading every book they could and attending conferences. Dave spent those years dialing in his recipes, some of which survived the transition to the brewery's portfolios of beers.

"Along the way, we found really amazing people in the industry who were the epitome of camaraderie," Wyndee said. "We were really drawn in by these people who didn't need to spend hours of their time reading our business plan or helping us out. We were really inspired by that camaraderie as they looked at others in planning as a rising tide floats all boats."

Eventually, though, a trip to the city of Henderson uncovered a fairly significant hurdle. At the time, there were two options for opening a brewery. One was opening a production brewery without a taproom, which defeated the Forrests' ideals of building a community around their business. To build a community around a taproom, however, would set them back $60,000 for a brewpub license—complete with gaming.

"You don't have to have it, you just have to pay for it," Wyndee said. "Instead, I became a registered lobbyist and wrote new licensing separating brewpub without gaming and reduced it to $10,000."

Wyndee then went to every city meeting for sixteen months, and before long, city officials began to realize the positive addition brewpubs can make to a community, looking at the many communities across the United States that have allowed them to flourish.

"It really does make a difference having the city on your side," she said. "In that year and a half of lobbying and writing new licensing, we made really good relationships within the city, and that has benefited us for these four years we've been in business."

At the time, Wyndee's task at the city wasn't finished, however. Their chosen location in an industrial park near Las Vegas Distillery and Grape Expectations provided a nice beverage trifecta; however, it wasn't zoned for retail sales. Sure, 95 percent of their business would be manufacturing and wholesale, but the 5 percent taproom sales would be incredibly important to their mission. With those percentages in mind, it also didn't make sense to pay retail square footage. Wyndee worked to rezone the entire industrial park and succeeded in about five months' time.

The brewery opened in September 2014 with two signature beers: IPA Resinate and Saison Evocation. The lineup by 2015 included fifteen beers CraftHaus packages throughout the year, with Resinate remaining its top seller.

"A lot of times, breweries will open and give you 12 beers," Wyndee Forrest told *Las Vegas Week* in 2014. "I'd rather have strong, consistent quality beers that are brewed true to style than a portfolio of eight so-so beers."

CraftHaus was also the beneficiary of being the first successful brewery crowd-funding campaign in Nevada. They set out to raise $20,000 in twenty-four days. The campaign worked, raising $26,000, but more than anything, Wyndee, a publicist by trade, saw it as a big public relations win, with more than 89 percent of the pledges coming from within Clark County, showcasing public support. Those pledgers are now immortalized within the taproom.

The road to opening CraftHaus was much more arduous than at most other breweries, an industry full of harrowing stories and lengthy opening timelines. Southern Nevada hasn't been the most welcoming environment for beer, but the Forrests persevered through the tribulations and are now the proud owners of a business carrying out their original mission. There were many points when they could have given up, but passion won out.

"We did it because we want to share quality beer with the community and have people be proud of what we're making for them and to share with their friends," Wyndee said. "It's in turn their story, and that's one of the coolest things to see in the taproom is one of our regulars sharing our story with pride to a newcomer.

"It's nice because I'm always shouting from the mountaintops, but when you see other people paying it forward for you, it's all worth it."

Demand has outpaced supply, but the Forrests are content with slow, manageable growth. They opened CraftHaus without going into debt and took out their first traditional loan to purchase a canning line more than three years into existence.

"It was the right time to do it," Wyndee said. "It's amazing how many more banks will give us money when we don't really need the money."

Through it all, Dave has kept a job as a valet at Green Valley Ranch Resort, a career he's held since his days at UNLV in 2001.

"I basically work CraftHaus all day, and then I go and actually work my valet job at Green Valley at night," Dave told the *Las Vegas Review-Journal* in 2017.

When CraftHaus released its Silver State Blonde Ale on Nevada Day 2017, all of the sportsbook bars at Station Casinos, including Green Valley Ranch, began carrying the beer.

"It's kind of come full circle," Dave told the *Review-Journal*. "I used to just share my home-brew with my colleagues, and now to have my product upstairs is really surreal. I still have to kind of pinch myself."

CraftHaus announced in September 2018 that it would open a second taproom in early 2019 in the Las Vegas Arts District, joining Hop Nuts Brewing, as well as beer bars such as Three Sheets Craft Beer Bar and Nevada Taste Site. The taproom won't include any brewing operation but will offer a more central location for Las Vegans to sample their beers.

"We have strong relationships with many businesses in the Arts District and are excited to help build a community," said Wyndee Forrest, co-owner and founder of CraftHaus. "We appreciate what has been created in the area and are honored to be welcomed in by such great business owners."

The Brewers

To lead the brewery at CraftHaus, the Forrests hired Steph Cope and Steve Brockman, two brewers from Australia. Cope had worked at western Australian production brewery Gage Roads, with a brewing degree from Edith Cowan University. Brockman was the head brewer at the Monk Brewery and Kitchen, also in western Australia, along with a degree from Edith Cowan University.

Prior to their joining CraftHaus, Cope and Brockman were the tandem behind Two Brewers Abroad, which took them across the western United States for a year, working at various well-regarded breweries: White Labs Inc. in San Diego; Cascade Barrelworks in Portland, Oregon; Crooked Stave Artisan Beer Project in Denver; and Upslope Brewing and Saints Brewing in Boulder, Colorado. The project also took the brewers to more than three hundred breweries, where along the way they met the Forrests. Despite initial hesitancies of moving to Las Vegas, Cope and Brockman joined CraftHaus, with Cope becoming the first female head brewer in Nevada.

"We knew it was a perfect fit from our first conversation with Steve and Steph; it was like we spoke the same beer language," Wyndee said in a 2014 press release announcing their hiring. "We share similar craft beer philosophies and travel experiences."

Wyndee said Cope and Brockman make up a perfect brewing tandem. Cope likes to hit targets while Brockman is more creative and likes to use culinary ingredients in the brewing process.

"It's a perfectly balanced brewing team," Wyndee said. "It was important for us to hire brewers with education and experience because we don't want to damage the industry by putting out less than the highest quality we can. The industry has been good to us, and we want to be good for it."

Cope and Brockman left CraftHaus in the summer of 2018 to continue their beer journeys of the world.

Bad Beat Brewing

It's a story heard time and time again: an entrepreneur risking all his money on an endeavor. In Las Vegas, it only seems fitting that a brewery shares the common start-up story.

Nathan Hall and his wife, Sara, sold their house to help finance a brewery, launching Bad Beat Brewing in 2014 with $300,000. Bad Beat opened in July 2014 in Henderson's Artisan Booze District, several months before CraftHaus Brewery was able to open its doors.

Hall told the *Las Vegas Review-Journal* that the efforts by CraftHaus founders Wyndee and Dave Forrest were helpful to him setting up his operation with no debt.

Hall was a homebrewer for five years before he opened Bad Beat and brought on former Joseph James Brewing brewer Weston Barkley to help manage the ten-barrel brewing system. Themed around poker—Hall is a former player drawn to Las Vegas for the game—the brewery's main lineup of beers includes Bluffing Ain't Weisse, the Ringer Pilsner, Ante Up Amber, Hoppy Times and Gutshot. Even the name of the brewery, Bad Beat, refers to being an underdog in a game of poker and going all in, as Hall did with the brewery, and winning.

Hall gave Barkley control of the brewhouse and ability to change up recipes for better beer.

"When I turned 21, I had a hankering for beer, and eventually, I knew I wanted to do something with it as a profession," Barkley told the *Review-Journal* a year into the operation. "I like the freedom [Hall] gives me to design my own beers. This is what I've been working toward."

Bad Beat started its first brew, Gutshot Dry Irish Stout, and originally bottled its brews before moving to cans.

In 2018, Bad Beat was one of the local breweries to take a lead in brewing and releasing a wide variety of the trendy NEIPA, including one named for the fantastic season the Vegas Golden Knights had in their first year, called Garbage Idea to Put a Team in the Desert.

The Bad Beat taproom is smoke- and gaming-free and only serves up Bad Beat beers, guest taps, hard cider and soda. Some snacks are available, but

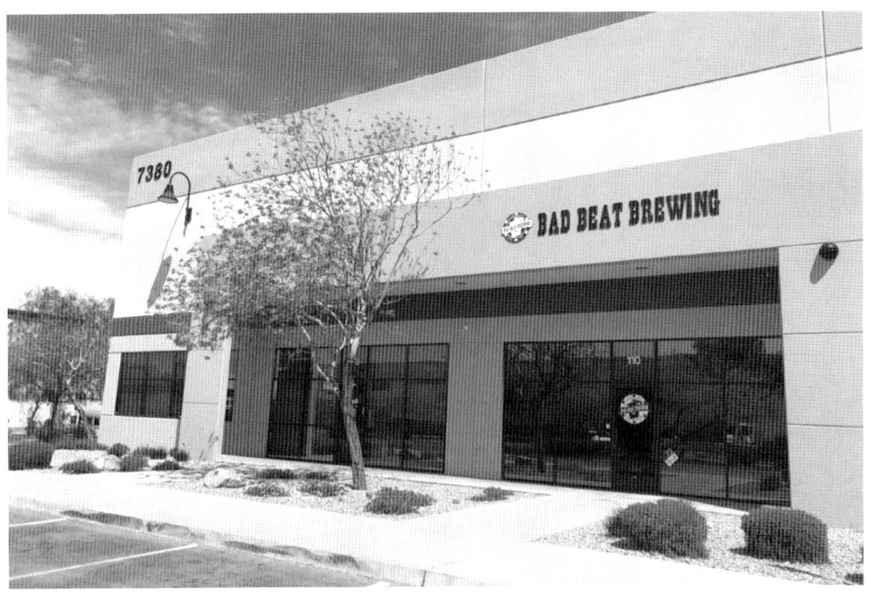

Bad Beat Brewing in Henderson's Artisan Booze District. The taproom is a short walk from CraftHaus Brewery and Las Vegas Distillery. *Photo by Pat Evans.*

rather than a full-service brewpub, Bad Beat allows customers to bring in outside food and invites food trucks to the parking lot.

Bad Beat also wants to foster a fun environment and offers an NES video game system, giant Jenga, shuffleboard, darts and card games.

ASTRONOMY ALEWORKS

The Artisan Booze District landed its third brewery in the second half of 2018 when Astronomy Aleworks opened. The ten-barrel brewery opened with a relative skeleton fermentor collection, as founder Matthew Brady understood the risk of growing too quickly in the modern beer industry. Brady was joined by his father, Matthew, and Dom and Tom Tancredi as founders.

Matthew Brady also likes to keep his beer styles relatively simple and untrendy, mostly letting the beers speak for themselves and allowing people to drink what they like. Astronomy's five core beers are a blonde, kolsch, West Coast IPA, German-inspired red, American hefeweizen and stout.

"We don't have an idea about beer," Brady said. "We brew whatever we want. I refuse to conform to any style. I hate beer nerds when it comes to stuff like that."

Allan Harrison joined the company to head up the brewing program along with Matthew Brady. Harrison was an accomplished, award-winning homebrewer prior to his turning pro. Brady started brewing with his parents when he moved to Las Vegas from Seattle in 2004 and has been ever since.

"I just kept up with it, and it's a cool damn job!" he said.

The design of the taproom—which, like CraftHaus and Bad Beat, offers a simple aesthetic akin to breweries outside Las Vegas—is dedicated to the science fiction of the middle of the twentieth century and space exploration, both subjects of great interest to Brady. Even his names carry the theme, such as Mars Red and Nova Stout.

Joseph James Brewing

In 2008, there was no large-scale brewing operation in southern Nevada, but there was a desire to change that status.

Joseph James Brewing got its start as Fox Brewing in 2007, when it delivered a case of soda to Whole Foods, as no brewing license had been issued yet. The brewery was founded by Matt Lisowski and his father, James, a lawyer, and the brewery's name eventually took the name of Matt Lisowski's second youngest sibling who has Asperger's.

The production brewery in Henderson brews nearly four thousand barrels of beer, all for distribution.

There were initially big plans for Joseph James. The company expanded distribution to fifteen states, and an article in the *Milwaukee Journal Sentinel* reported that a facility would open in Franklin, Wisconsin, to help produce beer for the eastern half of the nation, with plans to scale up to fifteen thousand barrels of beer annually. The brewery never opened.

In 2012, Miller International Inc., a nearly century-old clothing company based in Colorado, acquired Joseph James Brewing.

Citra Rye Pale Ale has been a boon for Joseph James Brewing, as it started as a simple group experiment to make a beer the brewers wanted to drink. With a fresh shipment of a buzzy hop called Citra, Kyle Weniger altered his homebrew SMASH pale ale recipe—which used Vienna malt and Cascade hops—and threw in some rye malt, two-row malt and Centennial hops on top of loads of Citra. Weniger won a brewhouse competition, and the brewery moved forward making Citra Rye, which has since become a familiar beer across Las Vegas on tap and on shelves. Joseph James also began experimenting with its sour beer program in 2013, according to a *Vegas Seven* interview with Matt Marino, the director of brewing operations. The sour program has grown significantly in the five years since.

Citra Rye was entered into the 2013 Great American Beer Festival competition and won a bronze medal, then received plenty of media attention, including from publications like *Men's Journal*, which called it one of the twenty best pale ales in America.

It was at the 2013 Great American Beer Festival that Matt Lisowski learned he had been let go by the new ownership group. Initially telling *Vegas Seven* magazine "There are no words," Lisowski later wrote to colleagues and friends: "I have been proud to be a part of Joseph James Brewing. I am currently looking for other opportunities in the beverage industry, and will let everyone know where I end up. Please continue to support Joseph James Brewing. They produce world-class beers, and only great things will come from this brewery. Thank you for everyone's support!"

Lisowski ended up heading to Fish Brewing Company in 2014 and becoming an executive vice president in 2015.

Following Lisowski's departure, operations tightened up and distribution was greatly reduced as the company refocused on its home turf.

Gold Buckle Brewing, the holding company that owns Joseph James Brewing, also bought Durango Brewing in 2015, the third oldest brewpub in Colorado, according to Westworld.com.

Joseph James won a gold medal at the 2017 Great American Beer Festival for Imperial Smoked Porter with Cacao Nibs.

Able Baker Brewing

At bars across town, Able Baker Brewing's humorous Atomic Duck IPA and logo, as well as several other delectable beers like Honey Dipped Stout, can be found. With a familiar name and clean branding, it can be a surprise that Able Baker has no taproom and no real brewery.

The name pays tribute to the first two test atomic bombs dropped at the Nevada test site, and the flagship IPA and the brand's mascot, Atomic Duck, play off a myth of a duck that survived the blasts.

James Manos and Randy Rhode launched Able Baker in 2017 after teasing beers and a potential home in downtown Las Vegas in 2015. Rather than give up when their initial plans stalled, the two founders continued and met with Marino, who had extra capacity at Joseph James Brewing. Joseph James allowed them to use the brewhouse and even helped the Able Baker brewers finetune their recipes on a large brewing system.

LOVELADY BREWING

As latchkey teens living with a recently divorced mother, Richard Lovelady and his twin brother, Robert, made use of their father's left-behind homebrewing equipment. The beer the pair made certainly wasn't special, but as troublemaking teens, they were satisfied. "This wasn't good stuff, but hey, it had alcohol in it," Richard said. "It's what we could get."

The Loveladys had grown up with their father brewing in the late 1960s and '70s. Richard's most prominent memory includes his father putting raisins in the bottles, resulting in refermentation and exploding caps.

Brewing ran in the family, but at the time, it wasn't a viable small business option, so the Lovelady brothers went down their separate career paths. Richard went to the University of California–Berkley for business before heading to Europe and earning his international business graduate degree. He hoped to work in import-export. Robert went on to UNLV for a degree in hotel and restaurant management.

It didn't take too long for Robert to suggest to Richard that they start a brewpub. Richard liked the idea, quit his job and went to the fermentation sciences program at the University of California–Davis.

"The great thing is, once you get through the coursework, you get to apprentice at a brewery, and I got to apprentice at one in San Mateo," Richard said. "They liked me so much they kept me on, but the brewer couldn't get me approval for the salary, so I stayed on as a busboy."

The short stint didn't last long. Six months later, Gordon Biersch Brewing called the head brewer and asked if he'd like a job at the new Las Vegas location for the growing chain. He declined but suggested Richard Lovelady. After six months of working at Gordon Biersch in San

Francisco, Richard made his way to Las Vegas to help build and open the new brewery.

He worked for Gordon Biersch for two decades, eventually working as a regional brewer and overseeing the work of six Gordon Biersch breweries across the country.

Then the itch struck the brothers again. For Richard, it was a normal life progression. Children grew up. With kids gone, his wife wanted to either move back to her native Oakland, California, or open a brewery.

"I looked at house prices in the Bay Area and I said, 'Nope,'" Richard said. "It was way cheaper to open a brewery in southern Nevada."

The Lovelady brothers had talked about it for years. For most of the talks, Richard always pushed it as too much work. Now was the time to strike.

They picked Henderson, where the family has deep roots. Their grandmother taught school at Henderson's Basic High School for forty years. The Loveladys' eldest brother was born down the street from where the brewery would end up being built.

"We wanted to bring back what I remembered it as when I was a kid: a little downtown community," Richard said.

The brewpub dream expanded beyond the twins now, with older brothers Jerry and Jeffrey joining, along with friend Mike Brook.

Thanks to the work in Henderson in respect to brewpub licenses done a few years prior by the Forrests at CraftHaus Brewery, licensing for Lovelady Brewing was easier than expected. Additionally, the Loveladys were given some excellent incentives that made a build-to-suit new building make more sense than leasing an existing retail space, Richard said.

Lovelady Brewing opened on April 1, 2016, in downtown Henderson at 20 Water Street. Richard handles the brewing, Robert handles the taproom and Jeffrey, the mustachioed older brother, is in charge of sales. Jerry, the eldest brother, kept his day job but works on maintenance projects during the weekends.

"It's just like any other family business," Richard said. "You get sick of each other, sure, but the funny thing is me and my older brother both lived in Las Vegas for twenty years, and I see more of him now than ever.

"It can be good and bad. I tell people it's the equivalent of herding cats."

With Richard at the helm of the brewhouse, he wanted to run away from his history at Gordon Biersch, not because he didn't respect and enjoy his time there and what the company did but because he didn't want his menu to imply he was simply brewing the same beers customers could get at a nearby and established brewery. He also, dating back to his homebrewing days, liked experimentation and wanted to get back to playing with beer. That's not to say the beers at Gordon Biersch weren't fun.

"The great thing about Gordon Biersch is you have to make the same beers over and over, so you get really good at consistency and knowing if one little thing changes, what happens to the rest of the beer," he said. "I loved my time there, and that kind of experience isn't something you can buy. But I knew all of my beers were going to be nontraditional or beers you don't find commonly."

His stable of beers includes Outbock, a hybrid bock/IPA with Australian hops. He experiments with kettle sours, and one of his most popular beers is 9th Island Pineapple Sour (Las Vegas is sometimes referred to as an extension of the Hawaiian Islands because of its huge Hawaiian population).

"That's what gets my juices flowing, being able to create new beers," Richard said.

Despite the historic struggles of craft beer in Las Vegas, less than two years into business and even on an early Thursday afternoon, Lovelady Brewing will have a steady stream of customers.

With lots of inroads to take in Las Vegas, there is plenty of fertile ground for Lovelady to capture in its journey to make business as profitable as can be. In 2017, the brewery brewed nearly two thousand barrels of beer. At the facility, Richard can achieve at least four thousand barrels of beer. Nearby, nearly twelve thousand units of apartments might be built in the near future, so the local taproom might generate plenty of business in itself. If not, tap handles around the city will continue to be sought, Richard said.

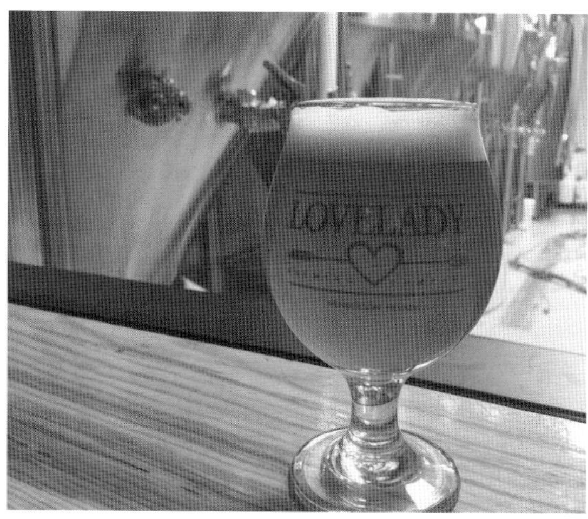

A beer overlooking the brewing space at Lovelady Brewing Company in Henderson. *Courtesy Lovelady Brewing.*

"Looking at the beer landscape now, it seems like the breweries in trouble are the breweries that are extending their reach too far," he said. "I don't want to dominate the local market, but I want to do really well here before I even think about going anywhere else."

Rather than having a mobile canning business come in to help package beers, Lovelady Brewing made the expensive investment in a canning line. Richard said it helps him know the product on the market is fresh. A mobile canning line could provide volume, but if it doesn't sell, it goes stale. Now, he is provided the luxury of packaging twenty cases, instead of two hundred, and sending it out to retailers who desire it.

Had Richard followed his original career choice into international business, he'd likely be a richer man. He doesn't look back. "My dream was to become an international business tycoon," he said. "I didn't like working in offices. I was good at it but didn't like it. Brewing is the perfect blend of creativity, physical and paperwork and drudgery. The great thing about it is, if you don't like what you're doing now, in thirty minutes you're doing something you do like."

Boulder Dam Brewing

Even when he owned his own business, Todd Cook hated Mondays, even dreading the morning as he prepped for bed on Sundays. Now, as the owner of Boulder Dam Brewing Company in Boulder City, he can't wait to get back to work on Wednesday following his one day off a week on Tuesday.

The power of beer.

Cook's life had taken him all over the world, first to a career in finance in London, England, and then into advertising, where he operated his own business for more than a decade. Eventually, work was enough and he, as he likes to put it, semi-retired. Living in Seattle as a single dad, he had some money put away and was enjoying the free time and exploring with his daughter. But an unexpected hobby took hold of his life.

He despised beer as a young adult, owing to a bad experience with what he believes was Coors. In college, he'd have the typical college brew every once in a while, but eventually he stumbled upon a friend a few dorm rooms down who had a refrigerator constantly stocked from the father's business trips to Europe.

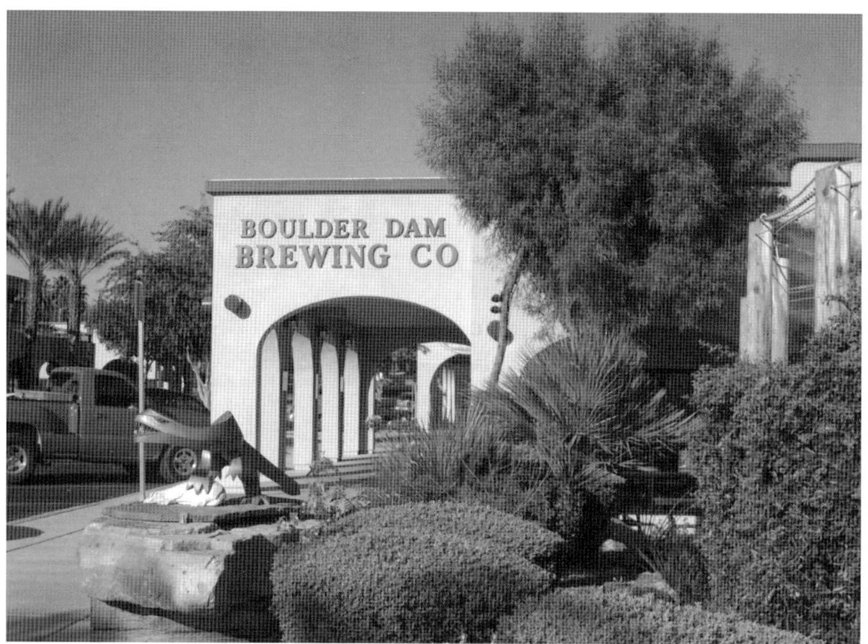

Boulder Dam Brewing Company opened in Boulder City, a once-dry community during the building of the Hoover Dam. *Courtesy Boulder Dam Brewing.*

He couldn't get enough of the imports. Then, in his early career move to London, he drank freshly brewed Guinness and, despite a prior belief that he wasn't a fan of dark beers, loved the creamy stout.

Back in the United States, after realizing finance wasn't for him, he started working at a bar. Following each shift, Cook received a shift beer, and he'd drink a Watneys Red Barrel, an imported mild ale from England. His manager suggested he try a beer brewed in America, but Cook declined, saying he didn't drink domestic beer. A few days later, he asked for his beer, and she gave him a beer in a pint glass. He recognized it wasn't Watneys but drank it anyway.

"It was really good, and it was Sam Adams Boston Lager," he said. "It was mellow and easy drinking with a lot of good character. I had gone through this progression of foreign beers, and finding a beer as good as imports was mind-blowing. I couldn't get enough."

With his newfound love, Cook would head to BevMo! and buy boxes of beer at single-bottle prices because he wanted to try as much as possible. He visited breweries every chance he got. Eventually, his friends noticed his passion, and one purchased him a $200 starter homebrew kit in 2002.

"That was it for me," Cook said. "Once I discovered all you have to do is follow recipes and as long as sanitation is good, you will make a good beer. A few years later, I started writing my own recipes and then started building this place less than six years later. It was a rapid progression."

The adventure to owning a brewery in Boulder City was a bit more of a complex path than his journey to owning a brewery. Living that semi-retired life in Seattle was good, but he couldn't stand the rain, nor did his father like his son not working. He told his dad all he wanted to do was brew beer, not at a brewery, but for himself. Being self-employed for more than ten years will make working for someone else a tough proposition.

One day, his father called him and told him to look at some tanks he had found online. His message was simple: "If you still want to brew beer, I'll go 50-50 in opening it with you as long as you buy me out in five years."

They started by looking in northern Arizona, but with his parents living in Boulder City, they noticed an empty building right on the main drag of the town. It was a three-year-old building, never occupied and a vanilla shell: no electrical or plumbing, just a sheetrock rectangle.

"I liked it a lot because it was downtown Boulder City and I didn't have to work around some other person's layout," Cook said. "I could build a thirty-five-foot bar, a kitchen there, a beer garden here. There were no preexisting limitations."

The resulting brewpub was much bigger than Cook originally planned. His original concept was more like Maritime Brewing's Jolly Rodger Taproom in Seattle, a frequent watering hole when he lived there. The little taproom sat eight at the bar, with a few high-top tables.

"That's what I wanted, a place I could brew in the day and bartend at night," Cook said, noting he still bartends on Saturday nights to stay close to his customers.

Instead, the Boulder Dam Brewing has turned into a community center of sorts, a full restaurant with seating for 150 and often hosting events. House-brewed beer accounts for 80 percent of the beer sold, despite also having twelve guest taps.

The brewery serves a constant lineup of Powder Monkey Pilsner, Hell's Hole Hefeweizen, Spillway Saison, Pekoe Pale Ale and Black I Stout, along with other seasonal selections. Cook still makes fewer than five hundred barrels annually, so far refusing requests to distribute Boulder Dam beer outside his walls. Maybe someday the beer will make it out, but he enjoys being a significant part of Boulder City's culture, and shifting attention away from the brewpub would hurt him internally.

"It's so much more than making beer," Cook said. "It's having entertainment, food, community events. It's a cool little town to be a big part of."

Originally, very little pushback was felt, Cook said. Aside from one person at city hall proclaiming, "I can't believe they're allowing a brewery in this town" when he received his license, everyone has been accommodating and enthusiastic about the establishment, he said.

The city, once home to the workers who built the Hoover Dam, has its brewpub for a population of fewer than sixteen thousand.

Maybe a month into business in 2007, Cook said a brewer came into the business and chewed him out, in the friendliest way possible. It was Dave Otto, the then-brewer at Big Dog's Brewing Company, and he was upset because the Las Vegas brewing community couldn't help support the opening of Boulder Dam because they didn't know it was opening.

"The culture is just fun," Cook said. "Brewers are so congenial, and they were upset because they weren't able to help me. That was when I found out we're all buds."

CHAPTER 14

RENO

Brasserie Saint James

Following great success running the Saint James Infirmary, Arthur Farley decided it was time to start making his own beer. Saint James Infirmary, a bar in Reno, was largely responsible for bringing in renowned beers to Reno, according to *Edible Reno-Tahoe*, helping further expand the already growing craft beer culture in the northern Nevada city.

Farley told *Draft Magazine* that when he opened Saint James Infirmary, he gave distributors a list of 100 beers, of which only 20 were already in Nevada. Eventually, he was serving 120 hard-to-find beers, but it still didn't satisfy his desires.

With that in mind, he set forth to open up a brewery concentrating on his preferred styles: European lagers, saisons and Belgian-style beers. In his bio on the brewery's website, Farley also notes he loves the "sparkling wines of France, Italy, Spain and North America, as well as the pinot noirs and Chardonnays of Burgundy, German Rieslings, Alsace pinot blancs, Cab Francs of Chinon and also America proud whiskey traditions."

Brasserie Saint James opened in the Crystal Springs Ice Company building, a former ice plant, in October 2012. According to *Northern Nevada Business Weekly* (*NNBW*), Farley knew immediately the building was the home to his future brewery when he walked through in 2010, two years after the water company left the historic building. He began demolition that year and began building the brewery in 2011, using found wood in the bar tops, tables and benches. "This was an old icehouse, and we found a treasure trove of wood that I could never have afforded to buy," Farley told *NNBW* in 2012.

All told, the $2 million investment paid off rather quickly, as Brasserie Saint James had wild success at the Great American Beer Festival in its early days, winning a 2014 gold and 2015 silver for Daily Wages, a saison. Using more than twenty yeast strains to contribute to the wide array of beers, Brasserie Saint James has won nearly forty awards since it started, including at that 2014 GABF, when the brewery also won Mid-Size Brewpub and Mid-Size Brewer of the Year. At the time, brothers John and Matt Watterson were at the helm of the brewhouse. Both had moved on to other breweries in different states by 2018. Madison Gurries was the brewery manager in 2018.

Before the brewery won the national award, it had already hit its annual brewing capacity of 1,200 barrels, according to Matt Watterson in a letter to the Nevada state legislature when he was director of the Nevada Craft Brewers Association. He was writing to encourage the legislature to increase the brewpub capacity cap of 15,000 barrels.

Along with being an award-winning brewery, Brasserie Saint James also concentrated on having a traditional array of food on the menu, reminiscent of a true French brasserie. Menu items include brasserie poutine, salmon rillette, fish and chips, Basque mussels and a brasserie burger, among many other items.

In April 2016, Brasserie Saint James opened a secondary taproom, called the Saint. The taproom houses the brewery's barrel-aged and wild brews, with twenty-four taps and doubling as a music venue.

Farley told Reno.com there were two main reasons the extension was opened: "We need a proper beer hall where the beer is the focus, and we need a barrel house so we can keep barrel-aging beer. I feel like I succeeded on my initial goal with Brasserie, but it did have some effects that I didn't foresee, which is that it is a brasserie—and it's the restaurant portion of the meaning of that word more than it is the brewery meaning of that word. So, people think of it and love it as a restaurant, but that kind of made the whole beer-hall thing go backseat to the restaurant. That was part of it, and also we just sort of ran out of room on the production side."

Brasserie Saint James did branch out of Nevada with a taproom and small brewery in San Francisco, opening in 2016. The location didn't last long and was officially closed in early 2018, with Farley citing a lack of "compelling revenue," according to Eater San Francisco. It wasn't for the lack of good product, as *SF Weekly* named it one of the best restaurants of 2016.

"Food is tough here," Farley told the website in January 2018. "We weren't fast casual but we weren't fine dining—to me, that's the market now. Slightly upper- to mid-tier restaurants just aren't en vogue right now."

Revision Brewing

Revision Brewing's roots stretch back to the University of Nevada, to a Californian garage and to California's Knee Deep Brewing Company, one of the nation's hot breweries from the past decade.

Jeremy Warren started his brewing life as a student at UNR before founding Knee Deep Brewing out of his Reno garage in 2010 with Jerry Moore. When the brewery started, the beer was brewed through a contract-brewing agreement in Lake Tahoe and initially distributed solely in the Reno area. In the ensuing several years, Knee Deep Brewing exploded into new distribution markets across the United States and earned critical praise from beer fans, driven in large part by Warren's IPA brewing prowess.

Warren left Knee Deep Brewing in 2015, citing creative differences with Moore.

"When I founded Knee Deep out of my garage six years ago there were things I set out to accomplish, and when I saw it wasn't going to happen with Knee Deep I realized it was time to move on to the next project," Warren told the trade publication *Brewbound* in January 2016. "This is my passion, this is what I love to do and it gets to a point—when you can't do [what you love]—it's time to move on."

In that 2016 *Brewbound* article, Warren was talking about the details of his next project, Revision Brewing, with an intended focus on IPAs, barrel-aged beers and sours.

"What I wanted to really get involved in was the barrel-aging and sour styles, and I wasn't able to get into that at Knee Deep," Warren told *Brewbound*. "When you talk about sours and barrel-aging, there's a lot of creativity, a lot of different styles that you can produce, and there's a lot of art and science behind it."

Warren initially looked at locations in California to continue his brewing career, even as he hoped to open the brewery less than seven months after the *Brewbound* article.

In May 2016, Warren detailed plans of a twenty-thousand-square-foot building in West Sacramento with plans to scale up to fifty thousand barrels to the *Sacramento Bee*. Those plans fell through by June 2016, and Warren exhausted options in the Northern California market before heading east.

Before a physical address and the ultimate decision to brew in Reno, Revision Brewing had distribution deals with at least five states.

Ultimately, Warren decided to return to his roots in Reno and, along with four partners, found a thirty-thousand-square-foot warehouse in Sparks and immediately invested $2 million into the project, according to the *Reno Gazette-Journal*. The original plans were to open a smaller satellite brewery in a secondary market, including possibly Reno, and according to the *Bee*, those plans weren't shelved with the relocation of the main brewery to Reno.

Revision Brewing set out from the beginning to be one of the powerhouse breweries of Nevada, with more brewing capacity than every other brewery in the state except Great Basin Brewing and Joseph James Brewing, according to the *Gazette-Journal*. According to a June 2016 *Brewbound* article, Warren planned to brew 5,500 barrels of beer—with head brewer and co-founder Jeb Taylor—and scale to 15,000 barrels within five years.

The initial brewing setup took up very little of the actual warehouse space, despite being a large setup for most modern start-up breweries, with a 20-barrel system and two 60-barrel fermenters, four 40-barrel fermenters and a 20-barrel fermenter. The Thirsty Nevadan noted that the brewery expected to scale quickly, with additions of five 80-barrel fermenters, four 120-barrel fermenters and four 60- to 80-barrel brite tanks. The Thirsty Nevadan reported that Revision expected to get between 10,000 and 18,000 barrels brewed in 2018.

Revision Brewing opened to the public in March 2017, with a grand opening in May, and began serving up an array of world-class IPAs, as expected from Warren's pedigree. Revision Brewing's year-round lineup includes Revision IPA, Revision Double IPA, What What Double IPA, Dr. Lupulin 3x IPA and Blonde NV Blonde Ale.

Warren's track record of tremendous IPAs continued at the 2018 World Beer Cup, when Revision won medals in the two most contested categories: American-Style India Pale Ale and Imperial India Pale Ale. Revision IPA won gold in the IPA category, while Revision Double IPA won silver in the imperial category.

Within its first year of operation, Revision Brewing also made waves riding the growing trend of hazy and Northeast-style IPAs with a whole line dedicated to special releases, including Disco Ninja (with Shoe Tree Brewing in Carson City), Tahoe Haze, Distance Haze, Jewel Box,

Planetary Fog, Planet Lovetron, the Bruff, Lord Lupulin, Smoke & Mirrors, Gimme Da Loot, Glitter Moon with Tiny Unicorns, Sparkle Muffin, Whole Lotta Ruckus, Trying to Get My Aroma, Bro, Battle of the Lords and Doyenne.

Silver Peak Restaurant & Brewery

Despite being talked about since the 1980s, it wasn't until 1999 that Silver Peak Restaurant and Brewery was opened by founders Dave Silverman and Trent Schmidt. The pair had met in high school and chatted since their teenage years about owning a business together. Schmidt graduated from UNLV with a degree in business management, and Silverman was a graduate of the Culinary Institute of America in Hyde Park, New York. Two of three aspects for a successful brewpub were taken care of, so Schmidt took on learning how to brew, including time at the original Karl Strauss brewery in San Diego, before finishing a formal brewing education at the Siebel Institute of Technology.

Opening in 1999, Silver Peak Restaurant and Brewery is one of the forefathers of Reno beer, despite opening several years after both Great Basin Brewing and Brew Brothers at the Eldorado Hotel and Casino.

In a 2017 *Reno News Review* column celebrating Silver Peak's status among the pioneers of Reno beer, Marc Tiar lamented the brewery's lack of innovation before acknowledging a solid lineup of beers and the full realization that it's just as much a restaurant. "With the utmost respect and recognition of their place in Reno's beer culture, I realize my epiphany today—Silver Peak is a restaurant that makes their own beer," Tiar wrote. "And they make good beer!"

The main lineup of beers at Silver Peak includes Red Roadster, XXX Blonde, Silver Peak IPA, Peavine Porter, Bailey Wheat Hefeweizen and Sierra Amber Ale.

A second location opened in 2004 when Silver Peak Grill and Taproom, now called River Peak, opened in downtown Reno.

Brewer's Cabinet

Now pegged with a flagship line of beers harkening back to Carson Brewing Company, the Brewer's Cabinet opened in 2012 as a tiny brewpub. It took an expansion to launch the Brewer's Cabinet's three Tahoe Beer brands, but they're now offered in attractive retro cans across the state.

The other beers from the brewery are also stellar, including Dirty Wookie, an imperial brown ale; Dragon Punch IPA; and Apparition Double IPA. The beer went statewide in distribution in 2017.

Brewer's Cabinet started with a three-barrel system inside the brewpub before expanding into an offsite brewing location in West Reno, which allowed them to brew plenty of the Tahoe brands, as well as can them, once the rights to the brand were acquired.

Michael Connolly, Chris Kahl and Zachary Cage don't just run a brewery; they also own several other establishments, including Legends Grill, Sports and Spirits, Sierra Tap House and Old Bridge Pub. Backed by those establishments, the trio was honored by the Reno Chamber of Commerce for the Reno Rebuild Project, which donates a nickel for every purchase from their establishments to help other businesses get their start in the downtown Reno area.

The Brewer's Cabinet opened a new taproom next to its main brewpub in the spring of 2018. The taproom was meant for overflow and allows guests to sample the beers without worrying about taking up restaurant space or waiting. The taproom has twenty taps—the restaurant only had twelve—which allows the brewery to offer the full lineup of beers, plus special releases and first tappings.

Under the Rose Brewing

As a homebrewer for six years prior to opening a brewery, Scott Emond knew from his very first batch that he wanted to be a professional. He studied as much as he could before getting a job at BJ's Brewhouse.

Under the Rose Brewing was started by Emond and his wife, Jesse Kleinedler, in 2013, both coming to Reno from the East Coast. When the brewery opened that year, it was likely a shock to future patrons. Emond's requirements for the brewery were a big bar, no TVs and an indoor bocce ball court, according to DrinkableReno.com. The interior of a body shop–looking building was full of games, tables of particleboard and a pit bull.

The brewery started with a ten-barrel brewhouse and four fermenters, but demand piled on early for Emond's innovative brewing program.

With the tagline "Crafted in Reno Beneath Mt. Rose," Under the Rose makes a huge variety of beers, ranging from the American-style Pale Ale Nevadabeer to Wicked Nor'easter, a sour New England–style pale ale. The beers offer an eclectic range of flavors. The brewery also makes an array of flavored blonde ales; Belgian-, British- and French-style ales; and a multitude of flavored porters.

In 2016, Under the Rose expanded into another location in midtown Reno. The new, smaller location is used to brew small batches of beers. "We'll crank out a ton of batches of all sorts of fun stuff—sours, fruited, spiced, honeyed—you name it, we'll use it in beer," Emond told the *Gazette-Journal*. "But since it's only seven kegs at a time, we can make those unique beers, and if it's not a fantastic hit, we can move on to something else."

Emond also said the midtown location would offer a new clientele—and wider base—than the Fourth Street redevelopments were offering at the time.

By 2017, the brewery was growing quickly, adding four twenty-barrel fermenters and two twenty-barrel brite tanks, according to TheThirstyNevadan.com. In 2017, production doubled that of 2016, and Emond told the Thirsty Nevadan, "In 2018, we expect to increase by another 5 times over this year."

Pigeon Head Brewery

In 2014, Pigeon Head Brewery opened up with the intention to be a mostly lager brewery with as much locally sourced ingredients as possible. Co-founder Eddie Silveira grew grain on his ranch in Yerington and intended to use it exclusively for some seasonal beers.

Opened in an old SPCA building under the Wells Avenue overpass on Fifth Street in Reno, the brewery launched with an India pale lager, pilsner, red rye ale and black lager.

Prior to opening, Silveira had met Lance Jergensen, who owns Rebel Malting, in a potential landing spot for his grain and ended up with a head brewer. Jergensen, along with being a malting entrepreneur, also had a long history of brewing, including a stint at craft pioneer New Belgium Brewing. Jergensen moved on to other endeavors, including helping launch Tonopah Brewing Company, a few years later.

In December 2017, the brewery changed ownership. Co-founders Silveira and James Mann sold the brewery to brewer Bryan Holloway, who had started with the company six months after it opened.

"Eddie and I never had intentions of selling this soon, but things have a funny way of working out for the best," Mann told TheThirstyNevadan.com, explaining that Holloway had asked for first rights on a chance to buy the brewery if the owners ever sold. With other businesses taking up the owners' time and another child for Mann, it eventually made sense.

"Obviously we wouldn't want to sell to just anyone, but Bryan would be a perfect fit because he was already making the beers and heavily invested time wise into the brewery."

Holloway and Peter Crooks took over and had big plans for the brewery. "I have plans to more than double our production within the next year and increase the volume of both keg and can sales," Holloway told the Thirsty Nevadan. "We are planning on distributing cans of seasonal and IPA selections in the near future, hopefully by this next summer. I want to keep rotating our seasonal as often as possible to give people something different every time they come in to our taproom.

"I am trying to put out beers that push the limits of innovation and are unique to the market."

StoneyHead Brewing

As a homebrewer, Paul Michelini would make an assortment of beers his friends would enjoy, so eventually it made sense to start a business, albeit a small one.

In 2013, Michelini opened StoneyHead Brewing with a one-barrel brewing system, not much larger than many homebrew setups, before moving up to a three-barrel system—small, but not too different from many brewery start-ups across the nation. Michelini opened the brewery all while continuing to work a day job, mostly just as a monetization of his passionate hobby.

The warehouse was fitted out with a couch, tables and a bar, all with the brewery in range to watch. "It's like homebrewing on steroids," Michelini told the website DrinkableReno.com.

His beers include the Galena Amber Ale, Honey Pale Ale, Sneak Attack IPA, Irish Red and a porter, along with a selection of seasonal like Summer Wit, a spiced wheat IPA.

THE DEPOT CRAFT BREWERY DISTILLERY

Few buildings in Nevada have the historic importance of the building the Depot Craft Brewery Distillery now calls home. Built in 1910 as the headquarters of the Nevada-California-Oregon Railway, the depot building was a hub for the state's ranchers and farmers.

As high school buddies Brandon Wright and Chris Shanks sought the home for their brewery, they were presented with many options, but few struck a chord like the depot. Justin Stafford was a third partner in the project but was out of the business by 2018. Despite the fact that the depot had been sitting vacant on Reno's Fourth Street for more than two decades and was in complete disrepair, the entrepreneurial duo saw past the building's shortcomings and into the future of a beautiful home for their combination brewery, distillery and restaurant.

"The building really settled on us because when we were presented the opportunity to acquire the building, it really felt like a no-brainer," said Wright, who manages the brewing and distilling operations. "We shopped around for several months, but this just instantaneously gave us a brand identity and a once-in-a-lifetime opportunity to build a brewery in a historic building."

With fourteen-plus-foot-high ceilings, original subway tile, light grain wood floors, a giant vault in the men's bathroom and plenty of natural light, the building looks much like it probably did in the early twentieth century, albeit with plenty of new materials from a months-long construction project.

The brewing and distilling systems are beautifully on display behind big glass windows behind the bar.

"The inside of the building is being designed to pay tribute to the original details while giving them an updated twist," Shanks told the *Reno Gazette-Journal* in 2014, before mentioning famed Nevada architect Frederic DeLongchamps. "The coolest thing is seeing a DeLongchamps building restored to its intended grandeur."

Wright likens the rehabilitation project of the building to restoring an old car—"you don't know what you're getting into until you get into it"—and said the building had a reputation among the city's developers as being a lost cause. As they ventured into the project, they did experience several hurdles of structural issues, including some extra steel support beams and twenty-six floor plans, but in the end, the building is now home to an elegant restaurant and taproom that opened on New Year's Eve 2014. Wright hopes the building—and business—will last another century.

The journey of Wright and Shanks dates back to their high school football days, which led to a lifelong friendship. In college, the pair shared a dorm room. Wright began homebrewing, and Shanks dove into the craft beer world, tasting beers from all over.

Combining his homebrewing with the jobs he started at sixteen at Reno's Silver Peak Brewing, Wright knew his future career path. Once he turned twenty-one, he enrolled in the World Brewing Academy, heading to the Siebel Institute in Chicago and Doemens Academy in Munich, Germany. Wright also attended the American Distilling Institute in Hayward, California. With his brewing degrees in hand, he was an assistant brewer for several years at Silver Peak before being promoted to head brewer for several more years. As a side gig, Wright would design brewhouses. An opportunity took him to San Diego to work for a consulting company helping breweries perform initial build-outs and expansions, including a project of a combined brewery and distillery, which he stored away in his mind.

He had the opportunity to open a brewery in San Diego, but there was a tug on his mind and heart: Reno. His long-term vision was to go back home, and that's when the business plan started in motion with Shanks.

With a degree in finance from the University of Nevada—Reno, Shanks eventually ended up in commercial real estate before helping turn around a restaurant in Reno. The partnership long talked about since the dorm room days seemed more and more like a match made in heaven.

"The job he did with the restaurant, it really impressed me," Wright said. "It really made me excited to start a business with him."

As the Depot approached its opening date, a law was in motion to allow for the sale of distilled spirits. Wright watched the bill closely—AB-153, he can still recall off the top of his head—and as soon as it passed, he knew they'd open as a brewery and distillery, the first such combination in the state.

"The place will be set up like a Willy Wonka factory," he told DrinkableReno.com in April 2014.

The main three-story depot building that houses the restaurant space and brewery is fourteen thousand square feet, but the company also occupies forty-seven thousand square feet of space in the surrounding buildings, which it uses for barrel aging and future expansion needs.

In its second full year of business, the Depot produced approximately 1,200 barrels of beer and sold about 1,000 cases of spirits. For Wright, who's at the helm of the operation, he wants people to be enamored with his products rather than simply drink them. A few years down the road, he'd much rather make 12,000 barrels of beer than 50,000 barrels of beer, a sentiment that might seem odd to people outside the brewing industry.

"It's been really fun making beers I want to make, and it's always been a dream of mine to be known for beers that are fun and not be a mass-adopted beer," he said. "We obviously try to have an approachable beer list in the taproom, but we try to have beers you can't get anywhere else, and we want to grow that into the spirits brands too."

Along with a standard lineup of beers like Voyager IPA, Ranch Hand American Ale, Explorer Pale and Blacksmith Stout, Wright has ventured into beers like the cantaloupe sour, smoked pilsner, double bourbon barrel-aged imperial red ale and rum barrel-aged imperial porter.

On the distilling side, Wright makes a range of spirits like Silver Corn Whiskey, Aged Corn Whiskey, bourbon, gin, aged gin, rye, single malt and Amer Depot, a liqueur with deep roots in Nevada made with local herbs, roots and spices.

Through the passion of local history, distilling, brewing and food in a unique setting, Wright and Shanks offer up a truly remarkable experience when it comes to hospitality in twenty-first-century Nevada.

IMBIB

IMBIB Custom Brews opened in June 2015 as the smallest brewery in terms of production capacity.

Matt Johnson, who is the president of the Nevada Craft Brewers Association in 2018, opened the brewery along with partners Bart Blank and Jason Green.

While the brewery focuses on sour and barrel-aged beers, IMBIB does make beers like IPAs, including a Freshy IPA Series serving up the style as it's meant to be: as fresh as possible, but in a revolving manner showcasing the many different types.

IMBIB also opened with the intention to make custom beers for events and homebrewers to brew their beer and leave it in the facility to ferment.

Behind the bar, the brewing facility is fully visible to patrons of the taproom and is loaded with barrels. IMBIB opened in 2015 with a 1.5-barrel brewing setup but took a massive upgrade in 2017, when it received a 10-barrel brewing system, along with two 10-barrel fermenters, two 20-barrel fermenters, two 10-barrel brite tanks and a 20-barrel brite tank for conditioning the fermented beers.

IMBIB made its sour beer prowess known at the 2018 Great American Beer Festival, when it took home bronze in the Berliner-Style Weisse category and silver in Belgian-Style Lambic or Sour Ale.

LEAD DOG BREWING

Fourth Street gained another brewery in 2017, when Lead Dog Brewing opened up next to the Depot, with then twenty-two-year-old Ryan Gaumer at the helm of the operation. Gaumer started brewing with his father at fourteen and continued brewing while in school at Pepperdine University, according to the *Reno Gazette-Journal*. Once he turned twenty-one, he began visiting breweries around the California college and started planning a brewery of his own following his sophomore year.

The building he settled on in his many visits back to Reno while in college was once planned to be a barrel taproom for Lake Tahoe Brewing, which went out of business after the owner ran into legal trouble.

Gaumer started the brewery with a fifteen-barrel brewhouse and began brewing his beers. Lead Dog's beers include Citra Solo IPA, Secret Stash NE IPA, Choconilla Stout and Peanut Butter Stout. The beers are distributed in Nevada and Northern California.

10 TORR

Blending science and brewing is not a strange story; in fact, it's downright smart. 10 TORR Distilling & Brewing Company, however, takes it to another level.

The brewery was founded after a visit to a 250-tap Mississippi bar in 2015. It was after an installation of refinery equipment by Nevada engineering firm Encore DEC. One of the engineers, Will Whipple, had been homebrewing for a decade and working at Encore for about six years when he ended up having a real conversation with Encore owner Randy Soule.

"The conversation developed into ideas then evolved into real thoughts about designing and building our own brewery and distillery that would produce products that were much more enjoyable than diesel fuel and gasoline," Soule told *Nevada Magazine*.

A former grocery store, built in 1940, was turned into a brewery and distillery with custom-made equipment.

Whipple brought in a second brewer, longtime brewing partner Melissa Test. According to Whipple and Test, the brewery uses vacuum distillation to keep the distilling process at a low pressure and room temperature for purer flavors, while the brewing process uses centrifuges for clear beers without stripping flavors.

10 TORR's beers include simple, clean beers like Secret Cove Cerveza and No Town Brown Ale but also trendy beers like the hazy IPA trio of Hazeron Collider, Hazemania Devil and Haze Wagon IPA.

The brewery opened in 2017 as Mill Street Still & Brew Taproom and Micron Beers but rebranded to 10 Torr in 2018. "We have decided to produce and distribute our beer and spirits under a single name—10 TORR. As we expand our product distribution to new markets outside of Northern Nevada we want to be more focused in our marketing," Whipple said in a 2018 press release. "Originally there was some confusion regarding our family of products. We are proceeding with the name that we believe defines the unique and best qualities of the products that we produce. 2018 is going to be an exciting year for us, we have many new beer and spirits releases on the horizon including canned craft cocktails."

ALIBI ALE WORKS

In December 2014, the first brewery on the Nevada side of Lake Tahoe in decades—at the very least, if ever—opened when Kevin Drake and Rich Romo opened Alibi Ale Works in Incline Village.

The two longtime homebrewers met through a network of homebrewers Drake had set up, first meeting at a potluck. Soon thereafter, the pair started homebrewing and sharing aspirations to start a brewery.

"He was definitely on more of a fast track than I was," Drake said. "I was happy with my life and job, but he talked me out of that quick, and we started writing a business plan." Drake had been homebrewing since the late 1990s but enjoyed his work as an environmental consultant, specifically dealing with water quality.

Romo had moved back to the Tahoe area from San Diego to be with his ailing father. "I was working in real estate development, and the bubble popped, so I lost my ass in real estate," Romo said. "My dad's fiancée asked me to move back, and a year turned into three years and I was needing to do something else."

At the time, Romo was making near six figures in HVAC, plumbing and electrical work, but he wasn't happy. His wife told him to pursue something he loved: beer.

In the summer of 2012, Romo and Drake wrote their business plan. They ran a Kickstarter campaign but failed to meet their goal, forcing them to step back and reconsider their idea.

"Our thinking at the time was a lot smaller," Drake said. "We had to figure out the scale we needed to make it real."

In North Lake Tahoe, there wasn't a lot of commercial real estate space, especially for a brewery to be any larger than a small brewpub, of which there were some on the California side. They wanted a production brewery and to be the first modern brewery packaging beer made with Lake Tahoe water.

The two finally found their building in a former auto parts and body shop in Incline Village in February 2014 and spent the rest of the year building out, with the skills of Romo's previous career and plenty of sweat from both of them.

Alibi Ale Works opened with a five-barrel brew system. It had only been open two weeks when the other tenant in the building left. Part of their plan was to eventually take the space, but not so quickly. It was either act or possibly lose out on that future idea. So they signed that lease and spent most of 2015 building out the space for a larger brewery, getting the fifteen-barrel brew system up in early 2016.

In 2017, Alibi Ale Works brewed approximately two thousand barrels of beer, with the capacity to do up to five thousand. Its beers are found in draft and in bottles and cans in the Reno-Tahoe-Truckee-Mammoth area.

There are lofty expectations for Romo and Drake, who desire to eventually find a space to open a brewery capable of fifteen to twenty thousand barrels annually.

"We've talked about it quite a bit," Drake said. "We'd like to have scale at a meaningful production level to get to markets we want without just growing in concentric circles. We'd like to have our beers in some of the most fun beer markets in the U.S., maybe half a dozen markets far from Tahoe."

Additionally, Alibi might be opening more taprooms in the near future.

"We really believe in that model," Drake said. "We like running taprooms. We enjoy that part of it in a market that is crazy competitive, for the ability to pour a lot of our beer over our own counters makes a lot of sense."

Carson City and Virginia City

With a rich brewing history, it's fitting that both Carson City and Virginia City have breweries in the modern craft boom.

Virginia City Brewery & Taphouse

No longer large enough to be home to multiple sizable breweries, Virginia City now has a population of fewer than eight hundred people, down from its 1800s peak of more than twenty-five thousand, and sustains 115 bars and saloons. The community certainly could have become a ghost town like many other early Nevada mining towns, but instead, it became a tourism hotbed for those seeking a vestige of the Old West and a deep arts community. Designated as a National Historic Landmark District, Virginia City attracts more than two million tourists every year, plenty of whom can be credited to the mid-twentieth-century drama *Bonanza*, set in the city.

Without Rick Hoover's efforts opening the Union Brewery in 1987, beer in Nevada likely would have been further delayed than its full passing in 1993, but his brewery ultimately stopped brewing in 1995, leaving a void in the historic city.

Following nearly twenty years of no active brewing in the historic city, three residents of the region, longtime piping, mechanical and HVAC professionals, acquired a building built in 1875 that once housed a restaurant and bakery and turned it into a grocery store and eventually a gift shop in 2014. The building now holds a fifteen-barrel brewing system, with four fifteen-barrel fermenters in a 1,300-square-foot building opened in 2015.

Beers brewed at Virginia City Brewery & Taphouse include 601 IPA, Steampunk Extra Pale Ale, YellowJacket Honey Pale Ale, C Street Wheat, Silver State Double IPA, Marlette Red and Dirty Mucker Stout.

Marc Tiar described the odd relationship of being a Renoite and visiting the faux Old West of Virginia City and his first experience at Virginia City

Brewery & Taphouse in a 2017 *Reno News and Review* article. "I really didn't have any expectations, but the 'Old West saloon meets modern brewery' was not surprising to walk into," Tiar wrote. "Situated in a prime spot on the main drag, the brewery is well positioned to cash in on tourists' Old West love and genuine high desert thirst. After some Old West touristing, you could do worse than to end your day with a pint here."

Shoe Tree Brewing

Residents of Carson City since 1992, brothers Jeff and Paul Young began homebrewing in 2008. Prior to their brewing days, they both embarked on different career paths. Jeff Young began drilling water wells in 2001 but was laid off in 2010. With nothing else to do, and with his newfound love of homebrewing, he turned to volunteering at High Sierra Brewing Company, a brewery then operating in Carson City. Within a month, he was offered a job, and within two years, he was the head brewer.

Paul Young, meanwhile, was at Carson High School until 2005 and then attended the University of Nevada–Reno, earning his degree in business management. When he graduated from UNR, he joined his brother at High Sierra Brewing, eventually becoming brewery production manager. Together, the Young brothers won a gold medal at the Great American Beer Festival for their Buzzed Bee Honey Ale. Six months after the major award, High Sierra Brewing ceased its Carson City operations and moved to Reno, at which point the brothers chose to stay in their hometown.

The brothers acquired a building in late 2015 and were working on their own brewery by April 2016.

"We're nothing if not obsessive about beer," Jeff Young told *Carson Now* in March 2016 in an article that suggested an opening by July 2016.

In reality, Shoe Tree Brewing opened in March 2017 at the Carson Hot Springs in a small, 1,800-square-foot building. Within the brewery, which also includes a taproom, the Youngs have a small brewery, led by a seven-barrel brewhouse and four fermenters capable of six hundred barrels a year.

Despite brewing a small amount, Shoe Tree Brewing brews up a variety of beers, including Shoe Horn, a double IPA; Mocha Porter; American Brown Ale; Stoutacus Imperial Stout; Blonde Ale; Cherry Berliner Weisse; Couples Therapy; Mocha Nut Porter; Green Apple Sour; Amber Ale; Belgian Ale; Fuzzy Lemon Sour, a Northeast-style IPA; Atomic Bank Vault, a Northeast-style double IPA; and St. Peppermint Paddy's Day Stout.

"We want to offer a full spectrum of beers, both traditional and non-traditional," Jeff Young told *Carson Now*. "We appreciate the traditional English and German beers, but we also appreciate the new American styles."

Outside of beer, Shoe Tree Brewing also makes its own sodas and nitro coffee, which sold out its first weekend open.

The name pays tribute to an important piece of local culture, a tree once adorned with shoes along Highway 50. Vandals cut the tree laced with shoes in 2010, but another tree has since taken its place. The brewery, however, will provide a potentially more permanent foundation.

"We definitely wanted a name that was local and unique," Jeff Young told *Carson Now*. "People have personal stories about that tree, and some people were even married under it."

Shoe Tree took home a bronze medal in the American-Style Sour Ale category at the 2018 Great American Beer Festival.

CHAPTER 15

OUTSKIRTS

Like most everything else in Nevada, most of the state's breweries call the Las Vegas or Reno metro areas home. There are three outliers, however: Clover Valley's Ruby Mountain Brewing Company, in the far northeastern corner; Tonopah Brewing Company; and the Colorado Belle's house brewery in Laughlin.

RUBY MOUNTAIN BREWING

In the mid-1990s, Steve and Maggie Safford sought to diversify their 1,500-acre Angel Creek Ranch in Clover Valley, a lengthy valley in the expansive Elko County. Wells is the nearest town to the ranch, with a population of fewer than 1,500 people.

"We saw the growth taking place in the microbrewery business in the early 1990s and decided to take advantage of it," Steve Safford told the *Las Vegas Review-Journal* in 1999. "I had sampled many of the different beers in the brew pubs, and I thought mine was competitive."

The rustic farm locale is similar to the hot breweries in the eastern part of the United States but in a far more remote location.

The Saffords brought in a ten-barrel brewing system as an upgrade from their five-gallon kitchen setup and started making beer commercially, with significant critical success in the early stages. Steve had been homebrewing for more than two decades, after all.

In 1996, Ruby Mountain Brewing won a silver medal at the Great American Beer Festival for its Angel Creek Amber Ale. The same beer took bronze the next year. Ruby Mountain Brewing's other beers include the Wild West Hefeweizen, Bristlecone Brown Porter and Vienna-Style Lager.

Ruby Mountain Brewing's beers are distributed in northern Nevada and southern Idaho. Expansion struck fairly quickly, and Ruby Mountain Brewing added three twenty-barrel fermenters to its stock of four ten-barrel fermenters in 1998.

Ruby Mountain Brewing has gained notoriety through the years, earning mentions in publications as large as the *Los Angeles Times*.

Along with the beer, Angel Creek Ranch still produces hay and Black Angus cattle.

Tonopah Brewing Company

Fred and Nancy Cline opened Tonopah Brewing Company in Tonopah, approximately halfway between Reno and Las Vegas, in 2014. The pair had a brewhouse custom-built in Germany, with large copper pot-like tanks, rather than the modern stainless steel tanks.

The Clines, who also own two wineries in California, bought and restored the Mizpah Hotel in 2011—paying $200,000, the same price it took to build more than a century prior. This establishment was founded in the early days of the city, which was founded in part by some of Nancy Cline's relatives. Cline's grandmother Emmy Ramsey was a postmaster of nearby Goldfield, and her great-uncle Harry Ramsey owned the first saloon in Tonopah, according to a 2016 *Las Vegas-Review Journal* article. Harry eventually struck it rich in the silver mines. It seems more than fitting now, as Cline owns a brewery in the city.

Beer was certainly an important part of Tonopah's early days as a mining town. Established in 1900 with the discovery of silver, one of the city's first buildings and businesses was a brewery outlet for Wieland Brewery.

"The idea of the brewery came about as we familiarized ourselves with the history of the town and realized back in 1900, beer was the working man's champagne in this tough mining town," Nancy told *Nevada Magazine* in 2015.

Tonopah Brewing opened with an array of beers inspired by Nevada's immigrant history and brewed by Lance Jergensen, then also the brewer at Pigeon Head Brewery in Reno.

According to the *Reno Gazette-Journal*, the beer lineup included an Irish ale, Baltic porter, pilsner and English-style IPA.

Richard Weathers has since taken over as the brewer at Tonopah Brewing and also manages the business, taking charge of the barbecue served up alongside the beers. The barbecue is smoked in house in a slow smoker, using staves from red wine barrels.

The Clines have invested heavily in a town of a little more than two thousand residents, and according to Nancy, it's all to help restore the beauty of an old western town. "We want something that's authentic where people can experience something that's true," Cline told the *Review-Journal*. "Not Disneyland, not Las Vegas, not an illusion."

COLORADO BELLE

A brewery in a Mississippi riverboat–inspired building isn't something found often, especially in Nevada. But there is such an establishment in Laughlin, a city ninety miles to the south of Las Vegas. The hotel and casino sits on the Colorado River, the border between Arizona and Nevada, and its name harkens to the tradition of riverboat names.

Pints Brewery & Sports Bar allows patrons of the riverboat casino to enjoy some food and kick back with some beer. The name changed from the original Boiler Room Brew Pub, aptly named as the room is meant to resemble the boiler room of a Mississippi riverboat.

Colorado Belle's brewery won Great American Beer Festival medals in 1998 for its red and in 1999 for Boiler Room Dark Lager. Today, the beer lineup includes Rehab Red, Pint's Premium Golden Ale, What the Puck IPA, Jackass Stout, Bodacious Blueberry and the Wild Card Brew, a changing handle for the brewers to go wild.

CHAPTER 16

CHAINS

As beer grew as a popular cultural movement in the 1990s, several chain brewpubs popped up and began spreading across the country. Among them were Gordon Biersch and BJ's Brewhouse, two of the preeminent brewpubs that make their own beers.

BJ's Restaurant & Brewhouse

BJ's operates five locations in Nevada—three in the Las Vegas area and two in Reno-Sparks—including one of its regional breweries, which helps supply the nearly 180 nationwide locations with beer. Most BJ's locations don't actually brew in house, but the Reno location does and makes upward of fifteen thousand barrels of beer a year. The Reno location opened up in 2006, according to a company earnings report.

By the sheer function of brewing for multiple BJ's locations around the country, the Reno brewery is one of the largest in Nevada, a fact the company touts on its website.

GORDON BIERSCH

In Las Vegas, the state's only Gordon Biersch is located and has played a significant role in the Las Vegas brewing industry.

Initially, Gordon Biersch set up a brewery in Sunset Station, in Henderson, but eventually opened up a from-the-ground-up brewery, the company's seventh brewpub, on Paradise Road, two streets east of Las Vegas Boulevard. When it opened in 1997, the *Las Vegas Sun* noted, "Although Gordon Biersch enters an already seemingly flooded market of breweries, the northern California partners insist they have something unique in their new outlet."

The fourteen-thousand-square-foot facility still looks and feels like a modern brewpub in 2018, more than twenty years later.

The company set out to capture the 1.2 million people who lived in Las Vegas at the time; adding any of the 31 million visitors to the city would be an extra benefit. It was the first free-standing Gordon Biersch location and the largest facility brewing its then three signature beers, a pilsner, marzen and dunkel.

Gordon Biersch sold the Sunset Station brewpub to Station Casinos Inc. in 1998, and it eventually became Barley's.

The facility has the capacity to brew up to four thousand barrels of beer each year, some of which is sent to other bars and restaurants in Las Vegas. Two other local brewers got their start at Gordon Biersch: Richard Johnson from Sin City Brewing and Richard Lovelady, the head brewer at Lovelady Brewing.

The Las Vegas Gordon Biersch even won a World Beer Cup in 2014 for its traditional German-style Bock.

Today, Gordon Biersch does experiment well beyond its classic lineup of traditional German lagers. "It's like anything; you need to adapt or fade away," said Richard Lovelady. "Gordon Biersch has adapted beer wise, but still, there's something to be said for simple beers."

The hesitancy to evolve, especially near the Strip, is understandable. The Strip has come a long way, but Lovelady remembers brewing his first hefeweizen at the Las Vegas Gordon Biersch. "People wouldn't drink it because it was cloudy," he said.

CHAPTER 17

AN UNFORTUNATE END

Despite the incredible rise of breweries in the United States during the past four decades, especially the past ten years, the small businesses aren't immune to failure. The closure rate has greatly lagged the speed of breweries opening. Fortunately for thirsty Nevadans, the Silver State will likely be flush with locally brewed beer for years to come, unlike the years following the closure of Reno Brewing in 1958. Still, breweries have already come and gone in Nevada. Whether they were victims of poor business operation, bad market or some shady activities, their beers are no longer on the market in Nevada.

Copper Summit Brewing

In 2005, the *Reno Gazette-Journal* wrote a story about the disproportionate number of breweries in the state, skewed by tourists. The article detailed the boom of the 1990s and the eventual fall and balancing of the industry.

"But as the '90s wound down, the craft-brewing industry matured and a shakeout took its share of casualties," the *Gazette-Journal* wrote. A brewery owner in South Lake Tahoe, Jeff Walker, told the newspaper at the time that only one in three breweries survives.

The *Gazette-Journal* listed multiple breweries that had come and gone, including the Carson Depot, McWain's Brew Pub and Eatery, Tahoe

Mountain Brewery, Sierra Sage Brewing Company, Lake Tahoe Brewing Company and Copper Summit Brewing Company.

Copper Summit launched in 1996, making it the third brewery in the modern era of beer in Reno, joining Brew Brothers and Great Basin Brewing. Opened by Steve DePaoli, Mark Ernst and Chris Stevens, the brewpub offered up a Cajun- and seafood-inspired menu, according to a 1996 article by the *Gazette-Journal*.

The former homebrewers invested $500,000 into the brewery and saw an industry with plenty of growth potential. Upon opening, Copper Summit had plans to brew between 1,200 and 1,500 barrels of beer a year.

Each of Copper Summit's beers was named for a mountain or elevation-related term, like Mount Rose Red Ale, Himalayan Hefeweizen and Slide Mountain Stout.

Copper Summit closed in 1999, a "victim of declining sales," according to the *Gazette-Journal*.

Buckbean Brewing

Few closed Nevada breweries have as much of an Internet presence as Buckbean Brewing, a company that opened in 2008 and played well to the media and competitions.

In its first year, Buckbean Brewing took home a bronze medal at the Great American Beer Festival in German-style Schwarzbier for Black Noddy Lager. In 2010, Doug's Very Noddy 40th Birthday Lager won bronze at the World Beer Cup.

Buckbean Brewing announced its closure in 2008, despite several years of award-winning brewing and national media attention. Cost of business and the after effects of the Great Recession were the downfall of the brewery, according to owner Doug Booth.

"We locked into our lease at the peak of the economy, and when we opened it was the worse-case scenario for malts and hops—all the prices skyrocketed," he said in a release. "In the end we were understaffed and under funded."

Buckbean Brewing gave plenty of warning to fans and offered discounts in the waning days of business.

Great Basin Brewing Company took over the facility, which helped spur the growth of the oldest brewing company in the state.

HIGH SIERRA BREWING

In a building that once housed Stew's Brewery and Doppelgangers, a brewpub turned nightclub, High Sierra Brewing replaced the business in 2011.

In 2013, High Sierra Brewing took high honors, winning a gold medal at the Great American Beer Festival for its Buzzed Bee Honey Ale.

High Sierra Brewing was forced out of its lease in March 2014, and founder Jim Phalan took to Facebook to explain the situation, namely that the business couldn't afford rising retail rents. With the business out of a home, Phalan partnered with Baldini's Casino and opened the new brewery in December 2014, before owner Baldini's purchased the company outright.

With Phalan out of the business, it was announced in 2018 that Oregon's Occidental Brewing Company would take over the space and retain as a brewer Tim Mason, who had come on board with the original move from Carson City to Sparks.

"We really like the burgeoning brewing scene in the Reno/Sparks area," Occidental co-founder Dan Engler said in a press release. "It's a tight-knit community that's been very welcoming and I think we'll be a good complement to the beer scene here.

"There is a lot of cool stuff happening in Reno and we're excited to be part of this market."

Occidental provides Nevada with excellently brewed product, mostly in authentic German-inspired styles.

LAKE TAHOE BREWING

Lake Tahoe Brewing Company exploded onto the burgeoning northern Nevada brewing scene in 2015, first opening a brewery early that year in Carson City, in the original High Sierra Brewing Company building, but immediately embarking on a region-wide expansion.

Lake Tahoe Brewing was started by German-trained Michael Candelario, who spent time working at a brewery in Belgium before returning to the United States. He hoped to share his love of the Belgian style of beers with Carson City, along with wood-fired pizza.

The Carson City brewpub had a dozen or more beers on at a time, according to DrinkableReno.com, which Candelario also told he'd be happy if he brewed up to two thousand barrels in 2015.

Later that year, Candelario announced additional Lake Tahoe Brewing projects, including a wood-aging facility in Reno, complete with taproom; a taproom in Truckee on the California side of the border; and a tap house and restaurant in Fernley.

Less than a year later, the *Reno Gazette-Journal* reported Candelario had been arrested on a felony theft charge. He was accused of stealing $45,000 from Three Ranges Brewing, a brewery in British Columbia, Canada. Carson City sheriff detective Sam Hatley told the *Gazette-Journal* the department also found forged documents.

According to the *Gazette-Journal*, within the first three months of 2016, all four of Lake Tahoe Brewing's locations were closed. In January 2016, the Carson City location was closed and employees were laid off. The same month, the company was evicted from one of its leases in Reno and its unopened location in Truckee.

In February 2016, the brewery's website, LakeTahoeBeer.com, was disabled, and a "closed due to non-payment" sign was on the Fernley location's door.

"We made really bad decisions over-extending ourselves trying to open all the breweries," Candelario told the *Gazette-Journal* in March 2016.

The *Gazette-Journal* also reported potential legal action by Rob Curtis, the owner of a federal trademark on the name Lake Tahoe Brewing Company from businesses in California. Curtis had asked for a licensing fee but was never paid, according to the *Gazette-Journal*. Curtis and Eric Bledsoe operated Lake Tahoe Brewing Company in Tahoe City, California, and Crystal Bay, Nevada, from 1993 to 2005 and won a Great American Beer Festival medal for their Tahoe Stout in 1998. A *Gazette-Journal* review in 2002 suggested the Tahoe Red and also gave rave reviews of the food.

In June 2016, Candelario surrendered to authorities with two outstanding arrest warrants, according to the *Gazette-Journal*.

Old School Brewing Company

Despite having its name on the side of its 8,500-square-foot building well into 2018, Old School Brewing on Desert Inn Road in Las Vegas has been closed since November 2016 after two years of business.

Jim Wilson had been planning the business at least three years before he opened the new brewery in 2014. Prior to Old School's opening, Wilson spent seven years as head brewer at Barley's Casino and Brewing.

According to the *Las Vegas Review-Journal*, Wilson was a grandfather who wanted a family-friendly hangout for his grandchildren. He offered beers such as the Homeroom Hefeweizen, Pale Ale 101, Varsity Vanilla Porter, ABCD ESB and March Irish Red Ale, according to Eater Las Vegas.

AFTERWORD

As I wrapped up this manuscript, I realized it hadn't even been a year since I had moved to southern Nevada. Already trying to catch up on the history of Nevada brewing and cramming it into a book, I could hardly think about where the state's beer future was headed; it's hard enough to try to imagine where the U.S. beer industry is headed next week. Less than a month after arriving in Nevada, I met Bob Barnes, a retired teacher and beer writer for more than two decades and editor of *Las Vegas Food and Beverage Professional*. Not only was he gracious enough to offer me a gig writing for the magazine, but he's also lived in Nevada his whole life and knows the beer scene better than most. He definitely has a better grasp of where Nevada beer is headed, based on its past.

So here's Bob Barnes:

Up until the 1990s, Nevada was a beer desert, and one would have to search long and hard to find anything other than the mass-produced "yellow" lagers being churned out by the big three domestic breweries of Bud, Miller and Coors. At the time, breweries were legal but had to sell the beer to a distributor, not directly to its customers as brewpubs do, and consequently none were in operation. In 1993, Tom Young and the late Eric McClary, accomplished homebrewers, worked with others and successfully lobbied the Nevada state legislature to legalize brewpubs, but a clause was added that restricted the location of a brewpub in Clark or Washoe Counties to redevelopment districts. Shortly after the law was amended, Young and

McClary opened Great Basin Brewing Company in Sparks, just outside Reno, and Holy Cow! Casino, Café and Brewery (now renamed Big Dog's Brewing) opened just a few weeks later. Nevada had its first brewpubs in the modern age.

The year 1995 marked another change to the law regulating breweries, as Assembly Bill 594 allowed brewpubs to operate pretty much anywhere bars were allowed, which led to casinos entering the brewing business. The problem was the licensing for brewpubs was set at $60,000, which made it difficult for individuals without well-heeled investors to attain their dream of opening their own brewery.

Fast-forward to 2014, when two more Silver State brewing pioneers came to the rescue with another change in laws affecting the licensing of breweries, specifically in southern Nevada, as Dave and Wyndee Forrest managed to convince the City of Henderson to amend its brewpub licensing to a more modern and business-friendly amended tavern brewpub license. The new amendment separated brewpubs into two subcategories, gaming and non-gaming, reducing the non-gaming brewpub license initiation fee to $10,000, which helped launch a boom of craft breweries, including Dave and Wyndee's CraftHaus Brewery in Henderson, Nevada. Around the same time, the City of Las Vegas also revised its brewery operating license fee, slashing it from $75,000 to a semi-annual fee of $500 or 1 percent of gross income, whichever is higher.

Another limitation to Nevada breweries has been an archaic law limiting the production of beer to only 15,000 barrels, which thankfully was bumped up to 40,000 by the Nevada legislature in 2017. (However, a retail cap of 5,000 barrels was imposed.) While this seems to be a step forward, the eventual eradication of any cap remains the state brewers' ultimate goal, and it's actually pretty ludicrous to have any cap at all, especially when you consider that according to the Brewers Association, our neighboring state of Arizona has a huge cap of production at 250,000 barrels and Washington, Oregon, Utah and New Mexico impose no cap. Currently, none of Nevada's breweries have exceeded the former 15,000-barrel cap, nor have any approached the 40,000 limit, but that could be changing soon. Case in point is Revision Brewing in Sparks (suburb of Reno), which, after opening in the spring of 2017, after only one year of operation in the spring of 2018 had expanded its production capacity from 8,920 barrels to 13,650 barrels, equaling a growth of 52 percent. With distribution far and wide covering Nevada, California, Idaho, Washington, Georgia, North Carolina, Vermont, New York and even Australia, look for it to reach capacity in the near future.

The number of breweries in Nevada is still just shy of forty, well below our neighboring states, but in the past five years, nearly a dozen entrants have opened in the small cities of Tonopah, Virginia City, Incline Village and Carson City and in the larger metropolitan areas of Reno and Las Vegas. A promising fact is that nearly all of the new and established beer makers have expanded since opening and continue to do so as their fan base is built up and appreciation, demand and, consequently, sales for the hometown beer increases.

One of the reasons for the growth is how communities throughout the United States, and now including cities in Nevada, have embraced locally brewed beer in increasing proportions. Where just five years ago one would rarely encounter a local beer in a casino unless it was brewed on-premise in a casino brewpub, now the situation has been reversed, as it's more the norm rather than the exception to find two or more local brews pouring. And for good reason, for as more and more people of drinking age have grown up appreciating craft beer instead of the macro brews their parents grew up with, the casinos have had to keep up with their clientele's tastes. Plus, just about every beer connoisseur will jump at the chance to try a local beer while on vacation that he/she may never have the opportunity to try at home.

Another reason for the success of local breweries is the fact that pretty much all of the brewpubs do a brisk business in their restaurants and tasting rooms and support one another by carrying guest taps from neighboring breweries. Furthermore, several craft beer bars make it a point to support and carry brews from Nevada breweries, such as Yardbird at the Venetian on the Vegas Strip (which devotes all sixteen of its taps exclusively to Nevada brews), Three Sheets, Eureka! and 595 Craft in Las Vegas; and Beer NV, Ole Bridge Pub, the Eddy and Six Four Growlers in Reno.

Another factor that should serve to boost sales of local beer is the nation's growing love for all things local. In late 2017, the National Restaurant Association surveyed nearly seven hundred professional chefs on which food, cuisines, beverages and culinary themes will be hot trends on restaurant menus in the year ahead. The number one culinary concept favored by 74 percent of responders was hyper-local (e.g. restaurant gardens, onsite beer brewing, house-made items), and in the subcategory of alcoholic beverages, topping the list were culinary cocktails at 68 percent, followed closely by locally produced wine/spirits/beer at 67 percent, house-brewed beer at 56 percent and growlers/crowlers at 38 percent. This has already been seen in recent restaurant openings, such as Flower Child in Las Vegas, which serves nothing but local beer from CraftHaus, Joseph James and Tenaya Creek.

So, logical reasoning would suggest that more restaurant guests will seek out locally brewed beer in 2018 and the years to come.

As for the state of the quality of Nevada's breweries, one has only to look at its history of winning major brewing competition medals. Proof that Nevada breweries measure up quite well is that Nevada breweries, as of May 2018, have earned a total of eighty-three major beer awards—fifty-nine GABF medals and twenty-four World Beer Cup honors—and a bevy of other accolades. Leading the pack is Great Basin, which since its opening in 1993 has won more major brewing awards than any other Nevada brewery, garnering thirteen GABF and nine World Beer Cup honors.

In conclusion, while Nevada currently lags behind its neighboring states and most of the rest of the nation in showing love to local brews and has some catching up to do, the gap is gradually narrowing, and the aforementioned stellar quality of the state's breweries and the population's growing patronage of its brews paint a bright future for craft beer appreciation in the state of Nevada. And while there likely will not be the explosive growth seen at the turn of the century, the demand will continue, prompting a steady stream of start-ups adding to the number of breweries of all shapes and sizes gracing the brew landscape of the Silver State.

BIBLIOGRAPHY

Interviews with the following were conducted by the author specifically for this project, a related project or articles: Bob Barnes, Michael Borer, Matthew Brady, Clyde Burney, Todd Cook, Kevin Drake, Wyndee Forrest, Greg Hinge, Kevin Holder, Ronald James, Richard Johnson, Sarah Johnson, Richard Lovelady, Robert Nylen, Dave Otto, David Pascual, George Racz, Rich Romo, Robert Snyder, Kyle Weinger, Brandon Wright and Tom Young.

Beasley, Yvonne. "The Depot Will Make Beer, Booze on E. 4th." *Reno Gazette-Journal*, November 14, 2014. www.rgj.com/story/money/reno-rebirth/2014/11/14/depot-will-make-beer-booze-e-th/19035221.

BeerAdvocate. "Jeremy Warren, Founder and Brewmaster, Knee Deep Brewing Co." www.beeradvocate.com/articles/9210/jeremy-warren-founder-brewmaster-knee-deep-brewing-co.

Brewers Association. "Here Are Your 2017 Great American Beer Festival Competition Winners!" Great American Beer Festival. www.greatamericanbeerfestival.com/the-competition/winners.

———. "Jeremy Warren Knee Deep Brewing Co." June 12, 2015. www.brewersassociation.org/profile/jeremy-warren.

Corey, Alexander. "Odyssey to Opening of Brewery Began Three Years Ago." *Las Vegas Review-Journal*, February 23, 2017. www.reviewjournal.com/business/odyssey-to-opening-of-brewery-began-three-years-ago.

Dixon, Kelly J. *Boomtown Saloons: Archaeology and History in Virginia City*. Reno: University of Nevada Press, 2006.

Earl, Phillip I. "Reno Brewing Company Dates from 1902." *Henderson Home News*, *Boulder City News*, October 19, 1995.

———. "Stat Can Thank Brewer for Bowers' Mansion." *Reno Gazette-Journal*, May 10, 1987.

Farley, Cory. "A Few Wrinkles Still to Be Ironed in Tahoe Beer's Struggle." *Reno Gazette-Journal*, March 3, 1985.

Hall, Shawn. *Old Heart of Nevada: Ghost Towns and Mining Camps of Elko County*. Reno: University of Nevada Press, 1998.

Higdon, Mike. "Revision Brewing Building Largest, $2M Brewery in N. Nevada." *Reno Gazette-Journal*, August 4, 2016. www.rgj.com/story/money/business/2016/08/03/revision-brewing-take-sparks-storm-2m-brewery/87979392/e.

James, Ronald Michael. *The Roar and the Silence: A History of Virginia City and the Comstock Lode*. Reno: University of Nevada Press, 1998.

———. *Virginia City: Secrets of a Western Past*. Lincoln: University of Nebraska Press and the Society for Historical Archaeology, 2012.

KTVN Channel 2. "Old Railway Headquarters Given New Life as the Depot Craft Brewery and Distillery." January 20, 2015. www.ktvn.com/story/27888732/old-railway-headquarters-given-new-life-as-the-depot-craft-brewery-and-distillery.

Las Vegas Sun. "Strip to Get New Brewery." June 20, 1996.

———. "Sunset Station Brews Deal to Buy Gordon Biersch Brewery." February 17, 1998.

———. "Talented Team Brews Up Business in LV." August 5, 1997.

The Locals vs. Tourists Balancing Act. "Joseph James Brewing Company Founder Ousted by New Owners—Vegas Seven." October 21, 2013. vegasseven.com/2013/10/12/joseph-james-brewing-company-founder-ousted-new-owners.

Lothrop, Jane. "Former Knee Deep Co-Owner to Open Revision Brewing This Summer." Brewbound, January 21, 2016. www.brewbound.com/news/former-knee-deep-co-owner-to-open-revision-brewing-this-summer.

McGlaughin, Mark. "Truckee's Craft Beer Scene Exploded Way Back in 1876 with Opening of Massive Boca Brewery." *Sierra Sun*, n.d.

Millard, Arnold A., et al. *History of the Carson Brewing Company: "Nevada's Oldest Business," 1860–1948*. N.p.: Brewery Press, 1980.

Moody, Eric N., and Robert A. Nylen. *Brewed in Nevada*. Carson City: Nevada State Museum, 1986.

National Park Service. "Carson Brewing Company—Three Historic Nevada Cities: Carson City, Reno and Virginia City—A National Register of Historic Places Travel Itinerary." U.S. Department of the Interior. www.nps.gov/nr/travel/nevada/bre.htm.

Nevada Appeal. "Shoe Tree Brewery in Carson City Opens Its Doors." March 13, 2017. www.nevadaappeal.com/news/local/shoe-tree-brewery-in-carson-city-opens-its-doors/d.

Nevada Historical Society Quarterly 25, no. 3 (1982). "The Breweries of Nevada."

Nevada Magazine. "The Depot Craft Brewery & Distillery." nevadamagazine.com/home/inside-the-magazine/cravings/the-depot-craft-brewery-distillery.

———. "Tonopah Brewing Co." nevadamagazine.com/home/inside-the-magazine/cravings/tonopah-brewing-co.

Northern Nevada Business Weekly. "The Depot Craft Brewery Distillery Trio Brings Different Skills to Business." February 9, 2015. www.nnbw.com/news/the-depot-craft-brewery-distillery-trio-brings-different-skills-to-business.

Nvbeer.com.

Prince, Todd. "Ellis Island Starts Work on $10M Dining, Entertainment Venue." *Las Vegas Review-Journal*, July 7, 2017. www.reviewjournal.com/business/casinos-gaming/ellis-island-starts-work-on-10m-dining-entertainment-venue.

Reno Gazette-Journal. "Biltz Offers High Bid for Reno Brewery." October 14, 1958.

———. "L.V. Redfield Has Taken Over Reno Brewery, Declines Comment on Who Will Operate It." May 26, 1954.

———. "Reno Brewery Building Sold to Redfield." May 26, 1954.

———. "Reno Brewery Sold at Auction." October 13, 1958.

———. "Reno Brewery Still Is Offered for Sale." July 8, 1954.

Rietz, Erika, and Joshua M. Bernstein. "Brewery to Watch: Brasserie St. James." *DRAFT Magazine*, February 2, 2018. draftmag.com/brasserie-st-james-watch-farley.

Sacramento Healthy Living. "Knee Deep in Great Beer." www.sacmag.com/Sacramento-Magazine/January-2015/Knee-Deep-in-Great-Beer.

Salem, Frederick William. *Beer, Its History and Its Economic Value as a National Beverage*. N.p., 1880. books.google.com/books/about/Beer_Its_History_and_Its_Economic_Value.html?id=bLlBAQAAMAAJ.

Shemeligian, Bob. "Pub Plans Brewing." *Las Vegas Sun*, January 30, 1997.

Stout, Robert Joe. "'Thirstiest State in the Union.'" *Nevadan Today*, August 7, 1988.

Winter, Tom. "Northern Nevada's Hot Peaks and Cool Views." *Los Angeles Times*, June 7, 2009. articles.latimes.com/2009/jun/07/travel/tr-jarbidge7.

World Beer Cup. "Award Winners." www.worldbeercup.org/winners/award-winners.

Wren, Thomas. *A History of the State of Nevada: Its Resources and People*. N.p.: Lewis Pub. Co., 1904.

As well as the respective brewery websites, numerous articles cited in text from DrinkableReno.com, Vegas Seven, Las Vegas Weekly, the Thirsty Nevadan and dozens of archived articles from Newspapers.com.

INDEX

J

K

L

M

N

O

P

R

Y

ABOUT THE AUTHOR

Pat Evans is a writer based in Las Vegas, Nevada, and Grand Rapids, Michigan.

As a graduate of Michigan State University, Evans started his journalistic career in sports writing before switching to business news. He spent five years at the *Grand Rapids Business Journal* and also was the beer columnist at sister publication *Grand Rapids Magazine*, a role he still holds.

Following his move to Nevada, Evans became a freelance writer, contributing to a variety of publications both regional and nationwide. Evans is also a corporate historian, documenting company stories and helping them stay true to their heritage while progressing into the future. He can be reached at nevadabrews@gmail.com.

Nevada Beer is Evans's second book. He released *Grand Rapids Beer* in 2015.